and Poems HOLIDAY
RING

Chosen and Introduced by ADELINE CORRIGAN

Illustrated by Rainey Bennett

ALBERT WHITMAN & COMPANY

Chicago

ACKNOWLEDGMENTS

The author and publishers gratefully acknowledge permission to reprint:

"A Round for the New Year" Reprinted by permission of Harold Ober Associates
Incorporated. Copyright ©1960 by Eleanor Farjeon

"New Year's Hats for the Statues" is reprinted by permission of Charles Scribner's
Sons from THE SEA OF GOLD AND OTHER TALES FROM JAPAN by
Yoshiko Uchida. Copyright ©1965 Yoshiko Uchida

"I Have a Dream" Reprinted by permission of Joan Daves. Copyright ©1963 by
Martin Luther King, Jr.

"My People" Copyright 1926 by Alfred A. Knopf, Inc. and renewed 1954 by
Langston Hughes. Reprinted from SELECTED POEMS, by Langston Hughes,
by permission of the publisher

"The Prize Is Won" From the book MARTIN LUTHER KING: THE PEACEFUL
WARRIOR, 3rd Edition by Ed Clayton ©1968 by Prentice-Hall, Inc. Published
by Prentice-Hall, Inc., Englewood Cliffs, New Jersey

"Fire-Logs" From CORNHUSKERS by Carl Sandburg, copyright, 1918, by Holt,
Rinehart and Winston Inc.; renewed, 1946, by Carl Sandburg. Reprinted by
permission of Harcourt Brace Jovanovich, Inc.

"Nancy Hanks" and "Abraham Lincoln 1809-1865" ABRAHAM LINCOLN and
NANCY HANKS from: A BOOK OF AMERICANS by Rosemary and
Stephen Vincent Benet, Copyright, 1933, by Stephen Vincent Benet. Copy-
right renewed ©1961 by Rosemary Carr Benet. Reprinted by permission of
Brandt & Brandt

"'Peculiarsome' Abe" from ABE LINCOLN GROWS UP by Carl Sandburg,
copyright, 1926, 1928, by Harcourt Brace Jovanovich, Inc.; renewed, 1954,
1956, by Carl Sandburg. Reprinted by permission of the publishers

"Good Bishop Valentine" Reprinted by permission of Harold Ober Associates
Incorporated. Copyright ©1960 by Eleanor Farjeon

"The Spice Woman's Basket" Reprinted by permission of Faber and Faber Ltd
from THE SPICE WOMAN'S BASKET AND OTHER STORIES

For the Tellers of Tales
and the
Children Who Listen
to the Magic of Words
in the
Libraries and Schools
of America

Festival Stories

Contents

To the Reader

Our holidays and other special days in America are set apart within the circle of the seasons. They have special meaning—historic, patriotic, religious, personal—and are important in our lives. The holidays celebrate the round of the year from January to December, the earth from seedtime to harvest and to seedtime again.

Holidays are days of remembrance, honoring significant events as well as heroic persons, great ideas, and courageous leaders. Their celebration is the outward expression of affection, gratitude, and pride. We come together to praise, sing, dance, laugh, play games, and enjoy festive foods, from cherry tarts for Washington's Birthday to the "gingerbread horn for Christmas morn."

Our traditions, customs, and legends are woven into each holiday, like flower patterns in brocade. Days such as Saint Valentine's and Easter are the heritage from a history shared in many lands. Other special days represent more recent events and newer loyalties. Earth Day stresses conservation and respect for our natural environment. Martin Luther King's Birthday is a tribute to a hero of our own time.

Both old and new, holidays are a unifying force, they form cultural links between peoples. They bring us together in gracious celebration, they call attention to the oneness of our common humanity.

The spirit of this anthology is in tune with its title and echoes the sound of bells ringing out in celebration of our nation's past and its ever-present and diverse beauty. The brief introductions to the individual holidays provide background information and to some degree suggest subjects for added reading enjoyment. Prose and verse in the spirit of the holiday follow. Selections have been chosen from authors of many different backgrounds and interests. Each has appeal and unique quality.

It is my wish that these stories and sprigs of rhyme chosen from the holiday round may charm your ear and delight your eye as they have mine. Then, as the Red Queen said to Alice in *Through the Looking Glass*, "We shall be queens together, and it's all feasting and fun."

Adeline Corrigan

JANUARY

New Year's Day

OBSERVED ON JANUARY 1

Merry are the bells, and merry would they ring;
Merry was myself, and merry could I sing;
With a merry ding-dong, happy, gay, and free,
And a merry sing-song, happy let us be!

Waddle goes your gait, and hollow are your hose;
Noddle goes your pate, and purple is your nose;
Merry is your sing-song, happy, gay, and free,
With a merry ding-dong, happy let us be!

Merry have we met, and merry have we been;
Merry let us part, and merry meet again;
With our merry sing-song, happy, gay, and free,
And a merry ding-dong, happy let us be!

This jolly old jingle of the bells is in the spirit of New Year's Day, the first day of the year. It is a widely observed holiday, and around the world New Year's greetings are heard in almost every language.

In America as well as in most of Europe, New Year's Day is observed on the first day of January, according to the Gregorian calendar. January is named for the Roman god of gates and doors, of beginnings and endings. He is pictured with two faces, one that looks backward, the other forward toward events to come.

New Year's Day, and especially New Year's Eve, is a time for fun and laughter, parties, singing, and dancing. Midnight is the moment when the old year ends and the new year begins. As bells ring out and whistles blow, people wish each other "Happy New Year!"

14

A Round for the New Year

Eleanor Farjeon

Round the ring around
Take each other's hands!
He who pauses in the round
Falls out where he stands.

Take each other's hands
Round around the ring —
Here we stand in winter-time,
Soon we'll stand in spring.

Round around the ring
As we go about,
Old Year pauses where he stands —
Old Year, fall you out!

As we go about
The ground begins to spin —
New Year can the fastest run,
New Year, come you in!

The ground begins to spin,
Spin with the ground,
Take each other's hands again,
Round the ring around!

New Year's Hats for the Statues

Yoshiko Uchida
adapted from Kasa Jizo

Once a very kind old man and woman lived in a small house high in the hills of Japan. Although they were good people, they were very, very poor, for the old man made his living by weaving the reed hats that farmers used to ward off the sun and rain, and even in a year's time, he could not sell very many.

One cold winter day as the year was drawing to an end, the old woman said to the old man, "Good husband, it will soon be New Year's Day, but we have nothing in the house to eat. How will we welcome the new year without even a pot of fresh rice?" A worried frown hovered over her face, and she sighed sadly as she looked into her empty cupboards.

16

But the old man patted her shoulders and said, "Now, now, don't you worry. I will make some reed hats and take them to the village to sell. Then with the money I earn I will buy some fish and rice for our New Year's feast."

On the day before New Year's, the old man set out for the village with five new reed hats that he had made. It was bitterly cold, and from early morning, snow tumbled from the skies and blew in great drifts about their small house. The old man shivered in the wind, but he thought about the fresh warm rice and the fish turning crisp and brown over the charcoal, and he knew he must earn some money to buy them. He pulled his wool scarf tighter about his throat and plodded on slowly over the snow-covered roads.

When he got to the village, he trudged up and down its narrow streets calling, "Reed hats for sale! Reed hats for sale!" But everyone was too busy preparing for the new year to be bothered with reed hats. They scurried by him, going instead to the shops where they could buy sea bream and red beans and herring roe for their New Year's feasts. No one even bothered to look at the old man or his hats.

As the old man wandered about the village, the snow fell faster, and before long the sky began to grow dark. The old man knew it was useless to linger, and he sighed with longing as he passed the fish shop and saw the rows of fresh fish.

"If only I could bring home one small piece of fish for my wife," he thought glumly, but his pockets were even emptier than his stomach.

There was nothing to do but to go home again with his five unsold hats. The old man headed wearily back toward his little house in the hills, bending his head against the biting cold of the wind. As he walked along, he came upon six stone statues of Jizo, the guardian god of children. They stood by the roadside covered with snow that had piled in small drifts on top of their heads and shoulders.

"*Mah, mah*, you are covered with snow," the old man said to the statues, and setting down his bundle, he stopped to brush the snow from their heads. As he was about to go on, a fine idea occurred to him.

"I am sorry these are only reed hats I could not sell," he apologized, "but at least they will keep the snow off your heads." And carefully he tied one on each of the Jizo statues.

"Now if I had one more there would be enough for each of them," he murmured as he looked at the row of statues. But the old man did not hesitate for long. Quickly he took the hat from his own head and tied it on the head of the sixth statue.

"There," he said looking pleased. "Now all of you are covered." Then, bowing in farewell, he told the statues that he must be going. "A happy new year to each of you," he called, and he hurried away content.

When he got home the old woman was waiting anxiously for him. "Did you sell your hats?" she asked. "Were you able to buy some rice and fish?"

The old man shook his head. "I couldn't sell a single hat," he explained, "but I did find a very good use for them." And he told her how he had put them on the Jizo statues that stood in the snow.

"Ah, that was a very kind thing to do," the old woman said. "I would have done exactly the same." And she did not complain at all that the old man had not brought home anything to eat. Instead she made some hot tea and added a precious piece of charcoal to the brazier so the old man could warm himself.

That night they went to bed early, for there was no more charcoal and the house had grown cold. Outside the wind continued to blow the snow in a white curtain that wrapped itself about the small house. The old man and woman huddled beneath their thick quilts and tried to keep warm.

"We are fortunate to have a roof over our heads on such a night," the old man said.

"Indeed we are," the old woman agreed, and before long they were both fast asleep.

About daybreak, when the sky was still a misty gray, the old man awakened for he heard voices outside.

"Listen," he whispered to the old woman.

"What is it? What is it?" the old woman asked.

Together they held their breath and listened. It sounded like a group of men pulling a very heavy load.

"*Yoi-sah! Hoi-sah! Yoi-sah! Hoi-sah!*" the voices called and seemed to come closer and closer.

"Who could it be so early in the morning?" the old man wondered. Soon, they heard the men singing.

> "Where is the home of the kind old man,
>   The man who covered our heads?
>   Where is the home of the kind old man,
>   Who gave us his hats for our heads?"

The old man and woman hurried to the window to look out, and there in the snow they saw the six stone Jizo statues lumbering toward their house. They still wore the reed hats the old man had given them and each one was pulling a heavy sack.

"*Yoi-sah! Hoi-sah! Yoi-sah! Hoi-sah!*" they called as they drew nearer and nearer.

"They seem to be coming here!" the old man gasped in amazement. But the old woman was too surprised even to speak.

As they watched, each of the Jizo statues came up to their house and left his sack at the doorstep.

The old man hurried to open the door, and as he did, the six big sacks came tumbling inside. In the sacks the old man and woman found rice and wheat, fish and beans, wine and bean paste cakes, and all sorts of delicious things that they might want to eat.

"Why, there is enough here for a feast every day all during the year!" the old man cried excitedly.

"And we shall have the finest New Year's feast we have ever had in our lives," the old woman exclaimed.

"Ojizo Sama, thank you!" the old man shouted.

"Ojizo Sama, how can we thank you enough?" the old woman called out.

But the six stone statues were already moving slowly down the road, and as the old man and woman watched, they disappeared into the whiteness of the falling snow, leaving only their footprints to show that they had been there at all.

Martin Luther King, Jr.'s Birthday

OBSERVED ON JANUARY 15

Hundreds of persons, black and white, crowded the rotunda of the Georgia State Capitol in Atlanta on January 15, 1974, for the unveiling of the portrait of Dr. Martin Luther King, Jr. This was the first black portrait in the state's official gallery, and Coretta Scott King, Dr. King's widow, referred to the occasion as a milestone in the recognition of her people.

The birthday of Martin Luther King, Jr., is warmly celebrated in many parts of the United States with memorial services and cultural programs. There is praise for the foremost Civil Rights leader who showed the way in the nonviolent struggle for racial equality. There is admiration for the character of a gifted man who spoke from his heart and moved people to action by his sincerity and eloquence.

Martin Luther King, Jr., was born in Atlanta on January 15, 1929, the son of the Reverend Martin Luther King and Alberta Williams King. He grew up in a family that read the Bible. The teachings of Christ were familiar to him from childhood. An excellent student who entered college at fifteen, he was especially interested in history, literature, sociology, and public speaking. He read widely in black history. He graduated from Morehouse College, Atlanta, and Crozer Theological Seminary, Chester, Pennsylvania. He received his doctor of philosophy degree from Boston University.

Ordained in the ministry, and married to Coretta Scott, Dr. King in 1954 returned to the South. He became pastor of the Dexter Avenue Baptist Church, Montgomery, Alabama. His success in the Civil Rights movement soon focused national attention upon him.

The young minister became interested in the life and philosophy of Gandhi, who by nonviolent methods worked for India's freedom. Gandhi had been influenced by the American writer, Henry David Thoreau, and so also was Dr. King. He admired the courage Thoreau showed in his essay "Civil Disobedience."

Dr. King believed in the goodness of man. He thought that Christ's teachings, the message of peace and brotherly love, and the ideas of Thoreau and Gandhi could be applied to the racial struggle for equality in the United States. He urged his followers to protest injustice in nonviolent ways.

In 1963, the centennial of the Emancipation Proclamation freeing the slaves, Martin Luther King led the famous march of 250,000 Americans in Washington, D.C. The marchers sought passage of a Civil Rights bill to insure all citizens the guarantees found in the Constitution of the United States and the Bill of Rights. The procession moved from the Washington Monument to the Lincoln Memorial, where Dr. King spoke. He shared his vision of a free and brotherly America where justice for his people and all people would one day prevail. This is the "I Have a Dream" Speech which moved listeners by the power and beauty of Dr. King's ideals.

The march in Washington was seen by millions on television and gave the Civil Rights movement new strength. When on July 2, 1964, President Lyndon B. Johnson signed the Civil Rights bill into law, Martin Luther King was a witness.

Leadership in the field of human rights won Dr. King the Nobel Peace Prize in 1964. He accepted the honor on behalf of all who love brotherhood and peace, and the audience rose in tribute to an American and an ideal.

Martin Luther King, Jr., only 39 years old, died on April 4, 1968, killed by an assassin. People remembered his words, "I've been to the mountaintop," and realized their truth. His work lives on.

I Have a Dream

Martin Luther King, Jr.

Five score years ago, a great American, in whose symbolic shadow we stand, signed the Emancipation Proclamation. This momentous decree came as a great beacon light of hope to millions of Negro slaves who had been seared in the flames of withering injustice. It came as a joyous daybreak to end the long night of captivity.

But one hundred years later, we must face the tragic fact that the Negro is still not free...

I say to you today, my friends, that in spite of the difficulties and frustrations of the moment I still have a dream. It is a dream deeply rooted in the American dream.

I have a dream that one day this nation will rise up and live out the true meaning of its creed: "We hold these truths to be self-evident; that all men are created equal."

I have a dream that one day on the red hills of Georgia the sons of former slaves and the sons of former slaveowners will be able to sit down together at the table of brotherhood...

I have a dream that my four little children will one day live in a nation where they will not be judged by the color of their skin but by the content of their character.

I have a dream today...

This will be the day when all of God's children will be able to sing with new meaning, "My country 'tis of thee, sweet land of liberty, of thee I sing. Land where my fathers died, land of the pilgrim's pride, from every mountainside, let freedom ring."

And if America is to be a great nation this must become true. So let freedom ring from the prodigious hilltops of New Hampshire. Let freedom ring from the mighty mountains of New York. Let freedom ring from the heightening Alleghenies of Pennsylvania.

Let freedom ring from the snowcapped Rockies of Colorado!

Let freedom ring from the curvaceous peaks of California!

But not only that; let freedom ring from Stone Mountain of Georgia!

Let freedom ring from Lookout Mountain of Tennessee!

Let freedom ring from every hill and molehill of Mississippi. From every mountainside, let freedom ring.

When we let freedom ring, when we let it ring from every village and every hamlet, from every state and every city, we will be able to speed up that day when all of God's children, black men and white men, Jews and Gentiles, Protestants and Catholics, will be able to join hands and sing in the words of the old Negro spiritual, "Free at last! Free at last! Thank God Almighty, we are free at last!"

My People

Langston Hughes

The night is beautiful,
So the faces of my people.

The stars are beautiful,
So the eyes of my people.

Beautiful, also, is the sun.
Beautiful, also, are the souls of my people.

The Prize Is Won

Ed Clayton

On October 14, 1964, Martin Luther King, Jr., took his place among the great men of all lands who have fought for the cause of peace. On that day, it was announced that the young Negro leader had won the Nobel Peace Prize.

The prize, which was first awarded in 1901, was named in honor of its donor, Alfred Bernhard Nobel, the Swedish chemist who invented dynamite. The Peace Prize is one of five Nobel prizes which are given each year that worthy recipients can be found. It is awarded "without distinction of nationality."

At thirty-five, Dr. King was the youngest person ever to win the award, and the second American Negro. The first was Dr. Ralph J. Bunche who won the Peace Prize for his work as a United Nations Under-Secretary.

The prize carries a cash award of $54,000 which Dr. King donated to the civil rights movement. The Nobel medal and diploma were presented to Dr. King in Oslo, Norway, on December 10, 1964, by Gunnar Jahn, the chairman of the Nobel Peace Prize Committee. The ceremony took place on the anniversary of Dr. Nobel's death in 1896.

Dr. King arrived in Oslo on a special chartered flight. With him were his wife, his father and mother, his brother and sisters and many of the civil rights leaders who had fought side by side with him for so long. Their memories of the long years of struggle were plain to see as they stood in the great hall of Oslo University. With pride, they watched a distinguished audience of world dignitaries, including King Olaf V of Norway, rise in a standing ovation for the simple Baptist minister from Atlanta.

In his presentation speech, Dr. Jahn described Dr. King as "an undaunted champion of peace...the first person in the Western World to have shown us that a struggle can be waged without violence." He spoke of Dr. King as one who has "suffered for his faith, been imprisoned on many occasions, whose home has been subject to bomb attacks, whose life and those of his family have been threatened, and who nevertheless has never faltered."

Dr. King's rich, compelling voice easily filled the huge hall as he acknowledged the award, saying: "I accept the Nobel prize for peace at a moment when twenty-two million Negroes of the United States of America are engaged in a creative battle to end the long night of racial injustice. I accept this award in behalf of a civil rights movement which is moving with determination and a majestic scorn for risk and danger to establish a reign of freedom and a rule of justice.

"I come as a trustee, for in the depths of my heart I am aware that this prize is much more than an honor to me personally... You honor the ground crew without whose labor and sacrifices the jetflights to freedom could never have left the earth.

"Most of these people will never make the headlines and their names will not appear in Who's Who. Yet when the years have rolled past and the blazing light of truth is focused on this marvelous age in which we live — men and women will know, and children will be taught that we have a finer land, a better people, a more noble civilization — because these humble children of God were willing to suffer for righteousness' sake."

FEBRUARY

Abraham Lincoln's Birthday

OBSERVED ON FEBRUARY 12 OR AS PROCLAIMED

Nancy Hanks dreams by the fire;
Dreams, and the logs sputter,
And the yellow tongues climb.
Red lines lick their way in flickers.
Oh, sputter, logs.
Oh, dream, Nancy.
Time now for a beautiful child.
Time now for a tall man to come.
"Fire-logs," by Carl Sandburg

On February 12, 1809, Nancy Hanks Lincoln gave birth to a son in a Kentucky cabin. She and her husband Thomas named the baby Abraham. When Abe was seven and his sister Sarah nine, the Lincolns set out for a new life in Indiana, but sorrow came in 1818 when the children's mother died.

The story of Abraham Lincoln, one of the great Presidents of the United States, is a tale of pioneer times and prairie life, woven of tradition and anecdotes. His cousin Dennis Hanks taught the young Abe to write, using a buzzard's quill. The boy liked school, but he had little of it. He read for hours, borrowing neighbors' books. "Raised to farm work," as he said of himself, he was kind to animals, enjoyed the outdoors, and could handle an ax, cut wood, and split rails. He had a way with words and he cared about people. Moving water attracted him, and he and his cousin John Hanks built and floated a flatboat down the Mississippi River to New Orleans. Not long after, he moved with his family to Illinois.

Young Lincoln left the farm to keep store, but his goal was to be a lawyer. He entered politics in Illinois and was elected to the state legislature when he was twenty-five. He became a successful lawyer, and in time he was sent to Washington to represent his state in Congress. In 1860, by then called "Father Abraham" and "Honest Abe," he was a candidate for President. Marching in torchlight parades, his followers sang, "Old Abe Lincoln came out of the wilderness, down in Illinois." When he was elected, crowds cheered him from each town as his train carried him to his inauguration.

As President, Lincoln never forgot the folklore of the road that had led from a pioneer home to the White House. He had a way with children and could shoot marbles and spin a top with his own little boys. He was a storyteller as well as a powerful speaker, using plain, forceful language.

He believed in the Constitution of the United States, and his belief was tested in the Civil War. Because of his leadership, the United States remained a single, strong nation. At Gettysburg where he dedicated a national cemetery on the site of a Pennsylvania battlefield, his short, moving address showed not only his faith in people but his hope "that this nation, under God, shall have a new birth of freedom, and that government of the people, by the people, for the people, shall not perish from the earth."

The war was almost over when, in his second inaugural speech, the President turned to the task of reuniting the North and the South, "with malice toward none, with charity for all." Only weeks later, Abraham Lincoln died, shot by an assassin. The memory of his greatness, however, remains ours today, and we therefore cherish his memory when we celebrate his birthday.

Nancy Hanks

Rosemary Carr and
Stephen Vincent Benét

If Nancy Hanks
Came back as a ghost,
Seeking news
Of what she loved most,
She'd ask first
"Where's my son?
What's happened to Abe?
What's he done?"

"Poor little Abe,
Left all alone
Except for Tom,
Who's a rolling stone;
He was only nine
The year I died,
I remember still
How hard he cried.

30

"Scraping along
In a little shack,
With hardly a shirt
To cover his back,
And a prairie wind
To blow him down,
Or pinching times
If he went to town.

"You wouldn't know
About my son?
Did he grow tall?
Did he have fun?
Did he learn to read?
Did he get to town?
Do you know his name?
Did he get on?"

Abraham Lincoln 1809-1865

*Rosemary Carr and
Stephen Vincent Benét*

Lincoln was a long man.
He liked out of doors.
He liked the wind blowing
And the talk in country stores.

He liked telling stories,
He liked telling jokes.
"Abe's quite a character,"
Said quite a lot of folks.

Lots of folks in Springfield
Saw him every day,
Walking down the street
In his gaunt, long way.

Shawl around his shoulders,
Letters in his hat.
"That's Abe Lincoln."
They thought no more than that.

Knew that he was honest,
Guessed that he was odd,
Knew he had a cross wife
Though she was a Todd.

Knew he had three little boys
Who liked to shout and play,
Knew he had a lot of debts
It took him years to pay.

Knew his clothes and knew his house.
"That's his office, here.
Blame good lawyer, on the whole,
Though he's sort of queer.

"Sure he went to Congress, once,
But he didn't stay.
Can't expect us all to be
Smart as Henry Clay.

"Need a man for troubled times?
Well, I guess we do.
Wonder who we'll ever find?
Yes—I wonder who."

That is how they met and talked,
Knowing and unknowing.
Lincoln was the green pine.
Lincoln kept on growing.

"Peculiarsome" Abe

Carl Sandburg

The farm boys in their evenings at Jones's store in Gentryville talked about how Abe Lincoln was always reading, digging into books, stretching out flat on his stomach in front of the fireplace, studying till midnight and past midnight, picking a piece of charcoal to write on the fire shovel, shaving off what he wrote, and then writing more — till midnight and past midnight. The next thing Abe would be reading books between the plow handles, it seemed to them. And once trying to speak a last word, Dennis Hanks said, "There's suthin' peculiarsome about Abe."

He wanted to learn, to know, to live, to reach out; he wanted to satisfy hungers and thirsts he couldn't tell about, this big boy of the backwoods. And some of what he wanted so much, so deep down, seemed to be in the books. Maybe in books he would find the answers to dark questions pushing around in the pools of his thoughts and the drifts of his mind. He told Dennis and other people, "The things I want to know are in books; my best friend is the man who'll git me a book I ain't read." And sometimes friends answered, "Well, books ain't as plenty as wildcats in these parts o' Indianny."

This was one thing meant by Dennis when he said there was "suthin' peculiarsome" about Abe. It seemed that Abe made the books tell him more than they told other people. All the other farm boys had gone to school and read "The Kentucky Preceptor," but

Abe picked out questions from it, such as "Who has the most right to complain, the Indian or the Negro?" and Abe would talk about it, up one way and down the other, while they were in the cornfield pulling fodder for the winter. When Abe got hold of a storybook and read about a boat that came near a magnetic rock, and how the magnets in the rock pulled all the nails out of the boat so it went to pieces and the people in the boat found themselves floundering in water, Abe thought it was funny and told it to other people. After Abe read poetry, especially Bobby Burns's poems, Abe began writing rhymes himself. When Abe sat with a girl, with their bare feet in the creek water, and she spoke of the moon rising, he explained to her it was the earth moving and not the moon — the moon only seemed to rise.

John Hanks, who worked in the fields barefooted with Abe, grubbing stumps, plowing, mowing, said: "When Abe and I came back to the house from work, he used to go to the cupboard, snatch a piece of corn bread, sit down, take a book, cock his legs up high as his head, and read. Whenever Abe had a chance in the field while at work, or at the house, he would stop and read." He liked to explain to other people what he was getting from books; explaining an idea to some one else made it clearer to him. The habit was growing on him of reading out loud; words came more real if picked from the silent page of the book and pronounced on the tongue; new balances and values of words stood out if spoken aloud. When writing letters for his father or the neighbors, he read the words out loud as they got written. Before writing a letter he asked questions such as: "What do you want to say in the letter? How do you want to say it? Are you sure that's the best way to say it? Or do you think we can fix up a better way to say it?"

As he studied his books his lower lip stuck out; Josiah Crawford noticed it was a habit and joked Abe about the "stuck-out lip." This habit too stayed with him.

He wrote in his Sum Book or arithmetic that Compound Division was "When several numbers of Divers Denominations are given to be divided by 1 common divisor," and worked on the exercise in multiplication; "If 1 foot contain 12 inches I demand how many there are in 126 feet." Thus the schoolboy.

What he got in the schools didn't satisfy him. He went to three different schools in Indiana, besides two in Kentucky—altogether about four months of school. He learned his A B C, how to spell, read, write. And he had been with the other barefoot boys in butternut jeans learning "manners" under the school teacher, Andrew Crawford, who had them open a door, walk in, and say, "Howdy do?" Yet what he tasted of books in school was only a beginning, only made him hungry and thirsty, shook him with a wanting and a wanting of more and more of what was hidden between the covers of books.

He kept on saying, "The things I want to know are in books; my best friend is the man who'll git me a book I ain't read." He said that to Pitcher, the lawyer over at Rockport, nearly twenty miles away, one fall afternoon, when he walked from Pigeon Creek to Rockport and borrowed a book from Pitcher. Then when fodder-pulling time came a few days later, he shucked corn from early daylight till sundown along with his father and Dennis Hanks and John Hanks, but after supper he read the book till midnight, and at noon he hardly knew the taste of his cornbread because he had the book in front of him. It was a hundred little things like these which made Dennis Hanks say there was "suthin' peculiarsome" about Abe.

Besides reading the family Bible and figuring his way all through the old arithmetic they had at home, he got hold of "Aesop's Fables," "Pilgrim's Progress," "Robinson Crusoe," and Weems's "The Life of Francis Marion." The book of fables, written or collected thousands of years ago by the Greek slave, known as Aesop, sank deep in his mind. As he read through the book a second and third time, he had a feeling there were fables all around him, that everything he touched and handled, everything he saw and learned had a fable wrapped in it somewhere. One fable was about a bundle of sticks and a farmer whose sons were quarreling and fighting.

There was a fable in two sentences which read, "A coachman, hearing one of the wheels of his coach make a great noise, and perceiving that it was the worst one of the four, asked how it came to take such a liberty. The wheel answered that from the beginning of time, creaking had always been the privilege of the weak." And there were shrewd, brief incidents of foolery such as this: "A waggish, idle fellow in a country town, being desirous of playing a trick on the simplicity of his neighbors and at the same time putting a little money in his pocket at their cost, advertised that he would on a certain day show a wheel carriage that should be so contrived as to go without horses. By silly curiosity the rustics were taken in, and each succeeding group who came out from the show were ashamed to confess to their neighbors that they had seen nothing but a wheelbarrow."

The style of the Bible, of Aesop's fables, the hearts and minds back of those books, were much in his thoughts. His favorite pages in them he read over and over. Behind such proverbs as, "Muzzle not the ox that treadeth out the corn," and "He that ruleth his own spirit is greater than he that taketh a city," there was a music of simple wisdom and a mystery of common everyday life that touched deep spots in him, while out of the fables of the ancient Greek slave he came to see that cats, rats, dogs, horses, plows, hammers, fingers, toes, people, all had fables connected with their lives, characters, places. There was, perhaps, an outside for each thing as it stood alone, while inside of it was its fable.

One book came, titled, "The Life of George Washington, with Curious Anecdotes, Equally Honorable to Himself and Exemplary to His Young Countrymen. Embellished with Six Steel Engravings, by M. L. Weems, formerly Rector of Mt. Vernon Parish." It pictured men of passion and proud ignorance in the government of England driving their country into war on the American colonies. It quoted the far-visioned warning of Chatham to the British parliament, "For God's sake, then, my lords, let the way be instantly opened for reconciliation. I say instantly; or it will be too late forever."

The book told of war, as at Saratoga. "Hoarse as a mastiff of true British breed, Lord Balcarras was heard from rank to rank, loud-animating his troops; while on the other hand, fierce as a hungry Bengal tiger, the impetuous Arnold precipitated heroes on the stubborn foe. Shrill and terrible, from rank to rank, resounds the clash of bayonets—frequent and sad the groans of the dying. Pairs on pairs, Britons and Americans, with each his bayonet at his brother's breast, fall forward together faint-shrieking in death, and mingle their smoking blood." Washington, the man, stood out, as when he wrote, "These things so harassed my heart with grief, that I solemnly declared to God, if I know myself, I would gladly offer myself a sacrifice to the butchering enemy, if I could thereby insure the safety of these my poor distressed countrymen."

The Weems book reached some deep spots in the boy. He asked

himself what it meant that men should march, fight, bleed, go cold and hungry for the sake of what they called "freedom."

"Few great men are great in everything," said the book. And there was a cool sap in the passage: "His delight was in that of the manliest sort, which, by stringing the limbs and swelling the muscles, promotes the kindliest flow of blood and spirits. At jumping with a long pole, or heaving heavy weights, for his years he hardly had an equal."

Such book talk was a comfort against the same thing over again, day after day, so many mornings the same kind of water from the same spring, the same fried pork and corn-meal to eat, the same drizzles of rain, spring plowing, summer weeds, fall fodder-pulling, each coming every year, with the same tired feeling at the end of the day, so many days alone in the woods or the fields or else the same people to talk with, people from whom he had learned all they could teach him. Yet there ran through his head the stories and sayings of other people, the stories and sayings of books, the learning his eyes had caught from books; they were a comfort; they were good to have because they were good by themselves; and they were still better to have because they broke the chill of the lonesome feeling.

He was thankful to the writer of Aesop's fables because that writer stood by him and walked with him, an invisible companion, when he pulled fodder or chopped wood. Books lighted lamps in the dark rooms of his gloomy hours....Well—he would live on; maybe the time would come when he would be free from work for a few weeks, or a few months, with books, and then he would read.... God, then he would read....Then he would go and get at the proud secrets of his books.

Saint Valentine's Day

OBSERVED ON FEBRUARY 14

Good morrow, Valentine,
First to thee, and then to mine,
So please give me a valentine.

Children chanted this old rhyme centuries ago on Saint Valentine's Day, and we still celebrate this holiday with gifts of candy, flowers, and fruit. Red hearts and Cupid, the winged boy with bow and arrow from Roman mythology, often decorate lacy cards that say "I love you."

The origin of Saint Valentine's Day is uncertain, but there are three traditions that contribute to its observance. One goes back to the ancient Roman festival, the Lupercalia, when young people chose their partners by lot, drawing names from a box.

Another tradition, from Roman history in the Christian era, is associated with two early Christian martyrs, both named Valentine, and both honored saints. Perhaps it is from the Saint Valentine who is said to have cured a child of blindness that there comes a legacy of love, especially for children.

The third tradition has to do with birds and their mating in the spring. Saint Valentine's Day was long thought to be the time when each bird found a mate. Samuel Johnson in his English dictionary of 1755 wrote, "Now all nature seem'd in love. And birds have drawn their valentines."

Whatever the true beginning may be, on February 14 we find roses are redder and violets more blue as we honor love and loved ones.

40

Good Bishop Valentine

Eleanor Farjeon

Good Bishop Valentine
Wandered all the night
Seeking out young lovers
And urging them to write:
With bags full of sugarplums,
Rose and violet bowers,
Hearts, doves, true-love knots,
And lace-paper flowers.

Good Bishop Valentine
By the moon's beam
Went seeking out young maidens
And urging them to dream:
With ribbons for their ringlets,
Love's silken strings,
Orange-blossom posies
And gold wedding rings.

Answer to a Child's Question

Samuel Taylor Coleridge

Do you ask what the birds say? The Sparrow, the Dove,
The Linnet and Thrush say, 'I love and I love!'
In the winter they're silent—the wind is so strong;
What it says, I don't know, but it sings a loud song.
But green leaves, and blossoms, and sunny warm weather,
And singing, and loving—all come back together.
But the Lark is so brimful of gladness and love,
The green fields below him, the blue sky above,
That he sings, and he sings; and forever sings he—
'I love my Love, and my Love loves me!'

The Spice Woman's Basket

Alison Uttley

"Nutmegs and Cinnamon,
Ginger and Caraway,
Spice from the Indies,
Buy, come buy."

The old spice woman sang this song as she walked down the street with her scented basket on her arm, and her staff in her hand. Wafts of sweet-smelling breezes from far-away islands came from her basket and floated around her. Invisible branches laden with flowers and tropical fruits swayed over her head. Blue seas lapped her feet, and the murmur of the waves accompanied her lilting chant. She felt none of these things, for they were dreams. Only a warm tide of happiness came from her heart.

In the King's kitchen there was a great cake-making. Mrs. Dumbledore, the cook, was making tea cakes, and when she looked in the wooden nutmeg box, it was empty. Through the open window she heard the voice of the old spice woman, and the rich smell of her wares came into the room.

"Run quickly and get a crown's worth of nutmegs," said she to the little kitchen maid, Betsy. "The spice woman only comes once a year, and I must have my box filled." She took from her fat purse a silver crown, and off trotted little Betsy in her wooden shoes clop-clopping across the palace yard, past the red-and-gold sentry who guarded the gate, to the old spice woman, who walked down the street, her basket on her arm and happiness in her heart.

"And what can I do for you, my dear?" she asked, holding out the basket with the starched white napkin lying on the top.

"A crown's worth of nutmegs for Mrs. Dumbledore, if you please, Mistress Spice," said Betsy, demurely, and she dropped a curtsy and held out her money.

The old woman put the nutmegs in a sugar-cone bag, and gave them to the dimpled girl. Then, with her blue eyes twinkling with merriment, she held out a little green nutmeg in her wrinkled hand.

"Here's a nutmeg for your own self, so keep it by you, my dear," said she kindly, and Betsy curtsied, and blushed, and ran back to the palace to Mrs. Dumbledore, who waited impatiently with her sleeves rolled up to her elbows and the nutmeg grater in her hand. Soon the tea cakes were in the oven, and when the Queen tasted them she vowed they were the most romantic cakes she had ever had.

But Betsy hid her own little nutmeg away in the tin trunk under the attic roof, and there it lay between her pocket handkerchiefs, waiting for her to take it home.

A year later the old spice woman came down the street with her basket on her arm. She had walked hundreds of miles up and down many a country since she had last been outside the palace, but never had anybody given her such a pretty curtsy, or spoken so nicely, as Betsy. She was thinking of her now as she sang:

"Nutmegs and Cinnamon,
Ginger and Caraway,
Spice for the Palace
Buy, come buy."

At that very moment Mrs. Dumbledore, with cheeks flaming from the kitchen fire, peered in the pewter cinnamon box.

"Goodness me! We've no cinnamon," she cried, throwing up her hands. "I have these cinnamon buns to make for Her Majesty, by special order, and there's nothing to flavor them. Take this crown, Betsy, and run out to the old spice woman before she gets away."

So Betsy upped with her little blue gown and ran as fast as she could, right out of the palace kitchen, across the yard, clop-clopping in her wooden shoes, past the tall grand sentry to the bent old woman, who walked the streets with the basket on her arm and happiness in her heart.

"And what do you wish for today, my dear?" she asked, and she held out the basket with its snowy linen on the top.

"A crown's worth of cinnamon sticks for Mrs. Dumbledore, if you please, Mistress Spice," said Betsy, and she curtsied and smiled at the old woman as if she were Her Majesty herself.

"Here's the cinnamon for Mrs. Dumbledore," said the old woman, as she wrapped up the golden-brown sticks in a paper, "and I am giving you a stick of cinnamon for your own self. Take care of it, my dear."

She held out a slender stick like a green branch, sweet-scented and rich, and Betsy thanked her, smiling and bobbing in her tucked-up blue skirt. Then back she hurried to the scolding cook, who soon made a batch of delicious cinnamon buns for the Queen.

Betsy carried her cinnamon stick upstairs, to the tiny room in the tower attic, and she put it at the bottom of her tin trunk with the nutmeg. She peeped through the narrow window at the red-roofed town below and the country beyond, for far away, over the distant hills, was the village where she was born. Then, with a sigh and a laugh, she sprang down the steep back stairs to the kitchen where there was much work to be done and no time to be wasted in thinking of her home and her mother.

Another year passed, a long weary year for Betsy. Mrs. Dumbledore was getting old and cross. Her face was redder than ever and her temper got shorter each day. Betsy ran from pantry to dairy, from storeroom to larder, but she could not go fast enough for Mrs. Dumbledore, who cuffed her and scolded her on all occasions.

It was the day for gingerbreads, and when Mrs. Dumbledore looked into the iron spice box where the ginger was kept, there was none. Everybody was most upset, for who can make gingerbreads without ginger, that hot spice which has a little fire in its heart?

Just then they heard a little quavering voice floating up from the street, coming like a sweet breeze through the window of the palace kitchen.

It was the old spice woman, with her basket of scented fare on her arm. She had trudged in far countries over the seas, in those islands of golden fruit and silver flowers, picking here and there, storing her basket ready for the cold lands where such things cannot grow. Her face was wrinkled as her own nutmegs, her arms were thin and dry as the spice she carried, but she lifted up her voice and sang in a shrill treble:

> "Nutmegs and Cinnamon,
> Ginger and Caraway,
> Spice for the Kitchen,
> Buy, come buy."

"Betsy, take this crown and buy ginger from the old woman. Run quickly, run!" scolded Mrs. Dumbledore, and Betsy hurried out of the kitchen, with her white cap awry, and her frilled apron tucked under her arm, and her little blue frock kilted round her, and her wooden shoes clop-clopping over the cobbled yard, past the fine sentry, through the great gates to the old spice woman, who was waiting in the street with her basket on her arm and love in her heart for the girl she remembered.

"What is your heart's desire today, my dear?" she asked, and she held out her spices with the clean cloth atop.

"A crown's worth of ginger for Mrs. Dumbledore, if you please, Mistress Spice," panted Betsy and she curtsied and smiled as if the old dame were the Princess of the Spice Islands herself, but her lips were trembling and her eyes were sad.

"Take this to Mrs. Dumbledore," said the old spice woman, who noticed the girl's trouble, and she wrapped the ginger in a leaf. "This is for yourself, a root of green ginger from the Land of Dragons. Keep it, for it may come in useful some day, my child."

Betsy thanked her and curtsied again. Then clutching the ginger in both hands she ran back to Mrs. Dumbledore in such a hurry that she lost one of her wooden shoes on the way, and Mrs. Dumbledore scolded her more than ever. So she went upstairs, up the long steep stairs, to the little attic. She put her green ginger at the bottom of her trunk, and then leaned from her narrow window, with arms outstretched towards home, but she could not see anything at all for the tears which dropped from her eyes. So downstairs she ran again, and started to work.

Now the next year, as you may have guessed, the old spice woman came again to the palace gates. She had travelled by blue water and green lands right round the world, seeking fresh spice and condiments. In all her travels she had never seen such a sweet maid as Betsy, for the old woman could look into people's hearts and read their secret thoughts. Her mind was stored with visions of scarlet and blue flowers, of glittering fruit, and bright birds, of mighty rivers and dark forests, and olive-skinned children who lived there, but the memory of Betsy was the best of all. She was a very old woman now, and she could sing only in a tiny voice, but the song came clear and true, like the voice of a bird, through the palace windows.

> "Nutmegs and Cinnamon,
> Ginger and Caraway,
> Spice for the Cottage,
> Buy, come buy."

It had been a sad day for Betsy. Mrs. Dumbledore had given her notice to leave, and she was to go home in disgrace, for who would hire a kitchen maid who had been dismissed without a reference by the Queen's own cook?

For the last time she was helping Mrs. Dumbledore to make cakes. Nothing was right. The palace cats had drunk the milk, the mice had nibbled the butter, and the spice box, the leaden spice box which had contained caraway seeds ever since anyone could remember, was empty. Mrs. Dumbledore said Betsy had eaten them all. The cook was in a raging fury, and Betsy was pale and anxious, for here was trouble even at the last moment.

Then they heard the fluting bird tones of the old spice woman out in the street, and the scent of the spices was in the air.

"Take this crown, and go quickly and buy caraway," cried Mrs. Dumbledore, giving the girl a push. "Be quick. No dawdling. Let me have no more carelessness on your last morning."

So Betsy ran out, and her little white cap fell off showing her golden hair all bunched up underneath it, so bright that the red-

and-gold sentry quite forgot his duty and stared after her. She ran clop-clopping past, with her hand outstretched and her pale pretty face eager to see the old woman again, as she walked up and down, with her basket on her arm and good fortune in her heart.

"And what is your wish today, my dear?" she asked, and she held out her basket which had nut leaves covering it.

"A crown's worth of caraway for Mrs. Dumbledore, if you please, Mistress Spice," said Betsy, and she curtsied and smiled at the old woman as if she were the Queen of Fairyland herself, but the curtsy was trembling, and the smile was only a flicker, and a tear rolled from each blue eye.

"Take this to Mrs. Dumbledore," said the old woman, holding out a hamper of caraway seeds, "but keep these for yourself. You'll want them very soon now." She gave the maiden a little packet wrapped up in one of the nut leaves, and Betsy put it in her pocket with many thanks. She wanted to throw her arms round the old spice woman and weep there, but she felt humble and shy. So, with the little brown hamper under her arm, she ran back across the courtyard, and as she passed the red-and-gold sentry he bowed and held out the white mopcap which she had lost.

"My heart," said he. "I mean, my cap," said he and then he stammered: "that is to say, your cap, my heart."

Betsy curtsied, confused, and took her cap with a shy glance at the tall young man who looked as fine as the King himself. Then on she ran to Mrs. Dumbledore with the caraway seeds, and her ears were boxed for her slowness in returning.

The ill-tempered cook made a hundred little caraway cakes for the royal tea table, but even before they were out of the oven Betsy had gone upstairs for the last time, to put her packet of seeds in the trunk and to lay her clothes neatly over them. She gazed out of the window, the narrow window up in the tower, and far away on the white highroad she saw a tiny figure gliding along, the old spice woman with her basket on her arm and her staff in her hand. Yet she walked not as an old woman, but with the sprightly step of a young girl, as if her troubles were over and she had slipped back again into youth, possessing its joys without its sorrows, its riches without its poverty.

The tall sentry, who was off duty, carried Betsy's tin trunk down the two hundred stone stairs, and put it in the carrier's cart, with never a word. Betsy rode away from the palace, jogging behind the white horse, home to the village where her poor mother dwelt.

Betsy had sent home every penny she could spare during her life in the palace kitchen, and now, with no money coming in, they had to live in extreme poverty. Nobody would hire a girl who had been turned away by the Queen's own cook, even though she could make angel cakes and queen cakes, saffron buns, and girdle scones. So Betsy earned her living by gathering and selling mushrooms and blackberries, or by marketing the produce of the little garden which surrounded the thatched cottage, the apples and plums and the bonny red roses and striped gillyflowers.

One day she thought of the spices which still lay at the bottom of the trunk in her bedroom. She brought them downstairs and showed them to her mother. They were as green as grass, and not fit to put in a cake, so she took them out to the garden and planted them in the little grass plot where she sometimes sat with her sewing in the evenings. She put them carefully in the deep earth, and watered them from the rain tub, and she gave a thought and a sigh to the old spice woman, Mistress Spice she had always called her, she reminded herself, but nobody knew what was really the name of the wandering magician with her basket of treasures.

A few days later she was astonished to see them sprouting, sending up little green-tasselled shoots, which grew at such a rate that in a month four bushy trees stood in the garden, with glossy leaves and exquisite flowers. The pink and white and rose-colored blossoms scented the whole village, and everyone came to lean over the hedge and stare at the strange foreign trees which had so miraculously grown.

Meanwhile at the palace things were going badly. The cakes were as heavy as stones and badly made, for there was no willing little kitchen maid to beat the eggs till they were light as a feather, to froth the cream, and to sieve the flour. The spice boxes of wood, pewter, iron, and lead were empty. Mrs. Dumbledore listened for the old spice woman, but she never came. The little song was no longer heard in the street, for the spice woman had gone on the longest journey of all.

The sentry in his red-and-gold uniform stamped angrily up and down before the palace gates, for he missed the sight of the merry little kitchen maid who was always too busy to glance at him. The Queen complained, and the King sent Mrs. Dumbledore packing, so nobody had any cakes at all.

Then the sentry thought it was time to take action. He marched out of the guardroom, and borrowed a horse from the royal mews. He rode over the hill and through the dale till he came to the village where Betsy lived. There she was, in her blue frock and white apron, standing on tiptoe, reaching up to her trees. Her gold hair was plaited round her head, and her blue eyes were fixed in wonder at the beauty of the flowers which covered the branches, just as the sentry's eyes were filled with amazement at the comeliness of the young kitchen maid in her mother's garden.

He tied the horse to the gate and went close to the hedge.

"My heart," said he, and Betsy turned quickly with a blush and smile and a curtsy, and went to her side of the hedge.

"My heart," said he again, but no other words would come. Then Betsy laughed softly to herself.

"It's you!" she cried. "Welcome in to see my trees!"

She showed him the four wonders. On one grew bright nutmegs, and another had twigs of cinnamon, and a third roots of ginger, and the fourth the brown seeds of caraway, yet all four at the same time had flowers of radiant beauty and heavenly perfume.

"My heart," stammered the sentry for the third time. "Her Majesty wants spice cakes, but no one can make them now Mrs. Dumbledore has gone, and the old spice woman never comes. The Queen's greatest desire is for spice cakes for the young princesses. If you will come back, just to make a batch of cakes for tea, it will cheer the palace and make everyone happy again."

So Betsy filled a basket with nutmegs and cinnamon, ginger and caraway, and rode behind the sentry, clasping his waist with her arms as the horse slowly ambled along. On the way the sentry suddenly found his tongue, and he told the girl all he had been thinking about since she went away, and he hadn't finished his tale when they arrived. It was a lovely story and Betsy's cheeks were red and her eyes bright as the fine sentry lifted her down at the palace gates.

The Queen took the spices and put gold coins in the basket instead, and then she filled the spice boxes with her own hand. She

52

asked Betsy to return and take the place of cross Mrs. Dumbledore as chief cake maker, but Betsy said she had already promised to be the red-and-gold sentry's wife. They were going to be married without delay, and they would live in the cottage with Betsy's mother, and each day the sentry would ride over the hills to guard the palace.

"Then I must get another cook," sighed the Queen, "but I will buy your spices, Betsy, for never have I tasted better. They are as aromatic as those of the old woman herself, and hers came straight from the islands of magic, I believe."

So Betsy returned to the cottage and watered her four trees. In a few days the sentry came riding on the bay mare, to take back a basket of spices and to see his Betsy. They spent the afternoon sitting in the shade of the trees, whose sweet fragrance floated around them, and whose flowers and fruit hung over their two heads bent close together.

As dusk fell there came a little shadowy old woman, soft stepping as a moth, singing like a distant nightingale, and the song she sang was:

> "Nutmegs and Cinnamon,
> Ginger and Caraway,
> Spice for true lovers,
> Buy, come buy."

She stopped in front of the two, and held out a shadowy basket. Betsy sprang from the sentry's arms and curtsied as she took it. She lifted the gossamer cover with trembling fingers, and the basket was full to the brim with Love. Before she could thank her the old spice woman vanished, and only a brown bird flew out of the garden and away to the starry sky.

Goldenhair

James Joyce

Lean out of the window,
    Goldenhair,
I heard you singing
    A merry air.

My book was closed;
    I read no more,
Watching the fire dance
    On the floor.

I have left my book,
    I have left my room,
For I heard you singing
    Through the gloom.

Singing and singing
    A merry air,
Lean out of the window,
    Goldenhair.

George Washington's Birthday

FEBRUARY 22
FEDERAL OBSERVANCE, THIRD MONDAY IN FEBRUARY

The greatness of George Washington is one of our proud possessions. For eight years he served as Commander in Chief of the Continental Armies as they fought the American Revolutionary War and won independence for a new nation. As the first President of the United States, he led his country in difficult times. A great and strong leader, he is worthy of the honor that is his today.

As a boy in Colonial Virginia, George Washington led a vigorous outdoor life. He swam, sailed, and rode horseback. He loved the earth and growing things and remained always a countryman at heart. He was proud to be a farmer, and Mount Vernon, his home on the Potomac River, was a particular pleasure to him.

Washington was a handsome, tall man, with a personality that commanded respect. Like his favorite brother, Lawrence, he was educated as a gentleman. He enjoyed people, parties, music, and hunting. He went to the theater, and play-reading was a favorite pastime with him. He liked fashionable clothes and dressed well. On his first appearance as Commander in Chief, he added a purple sash to his uniform and a rosette to his cocked hat. But for his inauguration as President he chose a simple suit, with eagle buttons, cut from American-woven brown tweed.

Much loved and much respected, George Washington lived to see his birthday widely celebrated by a grateful nation. There were parades and the firing of cannon, receptions, and birthnight balls at which the President, who was fond of dancing, stepped to the measured music of the minuet.

55

His sixty-seventh birthday, in 1799, was a happy family occasion. On that day at candlelight the stately general in his blue-and-buff uniform walked down the great hall at Mount Vernon with Nellie Custis, his adopted daughter, on his arm, to give her in marriage to his nephew, Lawrence Lewis.

In December of that same year George Washington died at his home in Virginia. For the memorial service, Congress invited General Henry Lee, the cavalry officer known as "Light Horse Harry" during the Revolution, to deliver the eulogy. His is the description of George Washington as "first in war, first in peace, and first in the hearts of his countrymen."

The capital city of the United States bears George Washington's name, as does the forty-second state to enter the Union. The greatest monuments to this hero's memory, however, are the integrity of his character and his powerful example of devotion to duty.

George Washington, The Torchbearer

Donald J. Sobol

At Fraunces Tavern, where General Washington said farewell to his officers, a visitor can still see Revolutionary flags and other mementos.

New York City wore a different look. During most of the year 1783 the docks had bustled with army commissaries selling surplus firewood, wagons, cattle, and horses. Over on Queen Street, loyalist merchants had auctioned off goods they could not take northward to their new homes in Nova Scotia or the valley of the St. John's River.

On Thursday, December 4, the chance to grab a bargain was forgotten. The city teemed with excitement. General Washington walked the crooked streets.

As the clocks struck noon he made his way among the old Dutch houses and the newer ones built in the Georgian style of England. The houses stood like momentous tombstones. Buried were the bonds of politics, loyalty, and affection for the Old World. The American flag flew over Fort George.

The people hurried to line his route. Heads poked from windows, handkerchiefs waved, and men dismounted and pulled their horses to the side. Some in the crowds longed to dart out and touch him, but did not dare. He was not a figure to fondle. He tilted his powdered head and smiled in the sober tradition of good manners by which he lived.

Turning west on Queen Street, he gravely mounted the curb and four steps and passed through the columned doorway of Fraunces Tavern to bid farewell to his officers.

It was to be a moment of highest drama, even as had been another moment at the very beginning, eight years before in Philadelphia. Then George Washington had sat wearing the red-and-blue uniform of his days as provincial colonel in the war against France. The uniform silently recommended to his fellow delegates to the Continental Congress that the time had come to fight. When John Adams had risen to nominate a Commander in Chief, Washington, forewarned, had not waited to hear his name. He had gone tensely from the hall that the other delegates might vent their opinions freely.

Afterward, he heard the details. Although unanimously elected, he had been the compromise candidate. "I do not think myself equal to the command," he told the Congress in his acceptance speech. He refused to accept pay beyond his expenses.

He spoke with Patrick Henry about his faulty qualifications.

He had not actively soldiered in eighteen years. His experience consisted of only five years of commanding small units in wilderness fighting.

To compensate, George Washington had limitless ambition, a love of right, and since early manhood a strong "bent to arms." He had found "something charming in the sound" of bullets tearing the air.

"Remember, Mr. Henry," the new Commander in Chief confided, "what I now tell you: from the day I enter upon the command of the American armies, I date my fall, and the ruin of my reputation."

If George Washington harbored a profound weakness, it was this fear of public disapproval.

Walking more slowly, Washington entered the long room of Fraunces Tavern. He moved to a refreshment table, summoning all his stony poise to conceal surging emotions. Awaiting his words in almost breathless silence were the officers who commanded the troops around New York, the last of a disappearing army.

His eyes brimmed. If he suddenly did not see the officers clearly, a corner of his mind could not have failed to total up those who must be absent. Gone were the almost-good-enoughs: Ward, Schuyler, Putnam, Charles Lee, Gates, and others who had arrived in 1775 with reputations that dwarfed their abilities, and they had left the scene early. Others had quit in disgust, broken by the strain of Congressional slowness or by jealousies of rank. Brave ones had died in the cause, and a few had been compelled to resign for reasons of health.

The long room was hushed. Washington fidgeted with a tidbit from the table. The faces watching him were a blur...The exquisite

boy, Lafayette, was away on a triumphal tour of his own. Greene...
Greene was in Newport, straightening out his muddled personal
affairs, but in war his head had been clearest. Of the host, Greene
alone with Washington had gripped the abiding truth: the army
was the Revolution. No engagement was to be risked if defeat
meant the capture or destruction of the army. Yet in the dark hour
after White Plains, Washington had conceived and Greene had
seconded the all-out risk that dealt the brilliant blow at Trenton.

Had Washington allowed Greene to rule him? True, the Commander in Chief listened to the Rhode Islander's counsel. But when
the grand opportunity came at Yorktown, Greene was away cam-
paigning independently in South Carolina. Washington and
Washington alone moved the army surely and rapidly to Virginia,
overseeing the complexities of supply and transportation.

Other men were his superiors in intellect and military training,
but none in patience, fortitude, and the willingness to learn. George
Washington mastered the art of war painfully. Personal wealth and
position notwithstanding, no one could lay better claim to the title
of self-made man.

Now, it was time for parting. In the still room Washington
abandoned the food with which he had been nervously toying. He
filled his glass with wine and raised it.

His hand was unsteady, his voice faltering as he spoke. "With
a heart full of love and gratitude, I now take leave of you. I most
devoutly wish that your latter days be as prosperous and happy as
your former ones have been glorious."

A low sound, a chorus of muffled grief, arose from the officers.
They drank their wine.

"I cannot come to each of you," said Washington haltingly,

"but I shall feel obliged if each of you will come and take me by the hand."

By apt chance, Henry Knox, of whom no commander could ask more in devotion and skill, stood closest. Their hands clasped. Overcome, Washington threw his arms around Knox and the two men embraced, kissed, and wept.

One by one the other officers, eyes wet and faces taut, stepped forward to receive the embrace that, having been given one, must be given all.

"The simple thought," wrote Benjamin Tallmadge, "that we were then about to part from the man who had conducted us through a long and bloody war, and under whose conduct the glory and independence of our country had been achieved, and that we should see his face no more in this world seemed to me utterly insupportable."

When the last officer had passed, Washington could bear the sorrow no longer. He stepped to the door, lifted his arm to the group, and strode from the room.

Outside he walked through an honor guard of light infantry, down Broad Street to the slip at Whitehall. Men, women, and children thronged to the wharf to glimpse the figure rare upon the face of the earth, a man of vision who was not a visionary.

He climbed into the barge made ready to carry him on the first leg of his journey home. As it shoved off, he turned once more to the officers who had followed at a respectful distance and now stood on the wharf. Again the gesture, the arm upflung like a torchbearer, a pose wholly unintended but truly the right of the man who had kept alive the light by which others had rekindled their hope, their courage, and their patriotism.

Homeward . . . Philadelphia . . . Wilmington . . . Baltimore
. . . and finally Annapolis, where Congress was sitting. Thomas
Mifflin tendered a dinner. Washington came as guest of honor,
though his host had been instrumental in the Conway Cabal of
1777, the shadowy plot to replace him as Commander in Chief.
Washington held no resentment. Never had he permitted personal
episodes to interfere with the national effort.

On December 23 he resigned his commission, "having finished
the work assigned me." He had led the American army for eight
stormy years, a period during which the British had changed com-
manders four times.

Before dawn he was in the saddle, a free citizen, relieved of his
stupendous burden. Hungrily he anticipated the days ahead—days
filled with picnics, clambakes, cards, billiards, fishing, duck-
shooting, horse racing, riding to the hounds...

Even as he rode south, the trumpet of recall was rising to the
lips of farseeing men. Six short years of rest and rebuilding his
plantation would be his, and then, before he could rest again, the
summons to eight arduous years as President. For it is a wise
country, it is said, that knows its own father.

As night fell on Christmas Eve in the year 1783 George
Washington cantered up the lane to Mount Vernon, bringing home
to Martha and to every American the gift of liberty.

Washington Monument by Night

Carl Sandburg

1

The stone goes straight.
A lean swimmer dives into night sky,
Into half-moon mist.

2

Two trees are coal black.
This is a great white ghost between.
It is cool to look at.
Strong men, strong women, come here.

3

Eight years is a long time
To be fighting all the time.

4

The republic is a dream.
Nothing happens unless first a dream.

5

The wind bit hard at Valley Forge one Christmas.
Soldiers tied rags on their feet.
Red footprints wrote on the snow...
...and stone shoots into stars here
...into half-moon mist tonight.

6

Tongues wrangled dark at a man.
He buttoned his overcoat and stood alone.
In a snowstorm, red hollyberries, thoughts, he stood alone.

7

Women said: He is lonely
...fighting...fighting...eight years...

8

The name of an iron man goes over the world.
It takes a long time to forget an iron man.

9

...   .
...   .

MARCH

Saint Patrick's Day

OBSERVED ON MARCH 17

Saint Patrick's Day honors the patron saint of Ireland, whose death is said to have occurred on March 17 in the year 461. In Ireland this is a time of thanksgiving for a loved person. Fresh shamrock is worn, and also sent abroad to friends. The world over, wherever there are Irish people or their descendants, the holiday is observed with parades, dinners, speeches, and cultural programs. Green is the color of the day, a salute to the Emerald Isle.

The man being honored was born about 385 in Roman Britain. As a young man he was captured by raiders and sold as a slave in Ireland. He escaped to France, where he became a priest and later a bishop. Returning to Ireland, he brought Christianity to the people, preached, built churches and monasteries, and introduced the Latin language. His unique self-portrait, written in Latin, glows with love and beauty.

Legends grew up around the saint's name. One says he plucked a shamrock to illustrate the mystery of the Holy Trinity. Even now, a hand bell believed to have been his can be seen in a jeweled box in the National Museum of Ireland.

Saint Patrick's Day calls attention to the cultural heritage of Ireland, to writers, poets, and storytellers who have enriched world literature. It honors the harpers, pipers, and fiddlers. It is an appropriate occasion to admire the art and calligraphy of one of the world's most beautiful books, the Book of Kells, in Trinity College Library in Dublin.

This is the time to tap the Irish crock of gold for stories and poems, from James Stephens, Seumas MacManus, Ella Young, Padraic Colum, Walter Macken, Patricia Lynch, and Eilis Dillon.

The Peddler of Ballaghadereen

Ruth Sawyer

Ruth Sawyer, author and storyteller, collected folk-tales in Spain and Ireland. Here is a story she heard from John Hegarty, a Donegal shanachie, or travelling storyteller. Ballaghadereen, which means "the road of the little oak wood," is a town in County Roscommon, Ireland.

More years ago than you can tell me and twice as many as I can tell you, there lived a peddler in Ballaghadereen. He lived at the crossroads, by himself in a bit of a cabin with one room to it, and that so small that a man could stand in the middle of the floor and, without taking a step, he could lift the latch on the front door, he could lift the latch on the back door, and he could hang the kettle over the turf. That is how small and snug it was.

Outside the cabin the peddler had a bit of a garden. In it he planted carrots and cabbages, onions and potatoes. In the center

67

grew a cherry tree—as brave and fine a tree as you would find anywhere in Ireland. Every spring it flowered, the white blossoms covering it like a fresh falling of snow. Every summer it bore cherries as red as heart's blood.

But every year, after the garden was planted the wee brown hares would come from the copse near by and nibble-nibble here, and nibble-nibble there, until there was not a thing left, barely, to grow into a full-sized vegetable that a man could harvest for his table. And every summer as the cherries began to ripen the blackbirds came in whirling flocks and ate the cherries as fast as they ripened.

The neighbors that lived thereabouts minded this and nodded their heads and said: "Master Peddler, you're a poor, simple man, entirely. You let the wild creatures thieve from you without lifting your hand to stop them."

And the peddler would always nod his head back at them and laugh and answer: "Nay, then, 'tis not thieving they are at all. They pay well for what they take. Look you—on yonder cherry tree the blackbirds sing sweeter nor they sing on any cherry tree in Ballaghadereen. And the brown hares make good company at dusk-hour for a lonely man."

In the country roundabout, every day when there was market, a wedding, or a fair, the peddler would be off at ring-o'-day, his pack strapped on his back, one foot ahead of the other, fetching him along the road. And when he reached the town diamond he would open his pack, spread it on the green turf, and, making a hollow of his two hands, he would call:

"Come buy a trinket—come buy a brooch—
Come buy a kerchief of scarlet or yellow!"

In no time at all there would be a great crowding of lads and lasses and children about him, searching his pack for what they might be wanting. And like as not, some barefooted lad would hold up a jackknife and ask: "How much for this, Master Peddler?"

And the peddler would answer: "Half a crown."

And the lad would put it back, shaking his head dolefully. "Faith, I haven't the half of that, nor likely ever to have it."

And the peddler would pull the lad over to him and whisper in his ear: "Take the knife—'twill rest a deal more easy in your pocket than in my pack."

Then, like as not, some lass would hold up a blue kerchief to her yellow curls and ask: "Master Peddler, what is the price of this?"

And the peddler would answer: "One shilling sixpence."

And the lass would put it back, the smile gone from her face, and she turning away.

And the peddler would catch up the kerchief again and tie it himself about her curls and laugh and say: "Faith, there it looks far prettier than ever it looks in my pack. Take it, with God's blessing."

So it would go—a brooch to this one and a top to that. There were days when the peddler took in little more than a few farthings. But after those days he would sing his way homeward; and the shrewd ones would watch him passing by and wag their fingers at him and say: "You're a poor, simple man, Master Peddler. You'll never be putting a penny by for your old age. You'll end your days like the blackbirds, whistling for crumbs at our back doors. Why, even the vagabond dogs know they can wheedle the half of the bread you are carrying in your pouch, you're that simple."

Which likewise was true. Every stray, hungry dog knew him the length and breadth of the county. Rarely did he follow a road without one tagging his heels, sure of a noonday sharing of bread and cheese.

There were days when he went abroad without his pack, when there was no market-day, no wedding or fair. These he spent with the children, who would have followed him about like the dogs, had their mothers let them. On these days he would sit himself down on some doorstep and when a crowd of children had gathered he would tell them tales—old tales of Ireland—tales of the good folk, of the heroes, of the saints. He knew them all, and he knew how to tell them, the way the children would never be forgetting one of them, but carry them in their hearts until they were old.

And whenever he finished a tale he would say, like as not, laughing and pinching the cheek of some wee lass: "Mind well your manners, whether you are at home or abroad, for you can never be telling what good folk, or saint, or hero you may be fetching up with on the road—or who may come knocking at your doors. Aye, when Duirmuid, or Fionn or Oisin or Saint Patrick walked the earth they were poor and simple and plain men; it took death to put a grand memory on them. And the poor and the simple and the old today may be heroes tomorrow—you never can be telling. So keep a kind word for all, and a gentling hand."

Often an older would stop to listen to the scraps of words he was saying; and often as not he would go his way, wagging his finger and mumbling: "The poor, simple man. He's as foolish as the blackbirds."

Spring followed winter in Ireland, and summer followed close upon the heels of both. And winter came again and the peddler grew old. His pack grew lighter and lighter, until the neighbors could hear the trinkets jangling inside as he passed, so few things were left. They would nod their heads and say to one another: "Like as not his pockets are as empty as his pack. Time will come, with winter at hand, when he will be at our back doors begging crumbs, along with the blackbirds."

The time did come, as the neighbors had prophesied it would, smug and proper, when the peddler's pack was empty, when he had naught in his pockets and naught in his cupboard. That night he went hungry to bed.

Now it is more than likely that hungry men will dream; and the peddler of Ballaghadereen had a strange dream that night. He dreamed that there came a sound of knocking in the middle of the night. Then the latch on the front door lifted, the door opened without a creak or a cringe, and inside the cabin stepped Saint Patrick. Standing in the doorway the good man pointed a finger; and he spoke in a voice tuned as low as the wind over the bogs. "Peddler, peddler of Ballaghadereen, take the road to Dublin Town. When you get to the bridge that spans the Liffey you will hear what you were meant to hear."

On the morrow the peddler awoke and remembered the dream. He rubbed his stomach and found it mortal empty; he stood on his legs and found them trembling in under him; and he said to himself: "Faith, an empty stomach and weak legs are the worst traveling companions a man can have, and Dublin is a long way. I'll bide where I am."

That night the peddler went hungrier to bed, and again came the dream. There came the knocking on the door, the lifting of the latch. The door opened and Saint Patrick stood there, pointing the road: "Peddler, peddler of Ballaghadereen, take the road that leads to Dublin Town. When you get to the bridge that spans the Liffey you will hear what you were meant to hear!"

The second day it was the same as the first. The peddler felt the hunger and the weakness stronger in him, and stayed where he was. But when he woke after the third night and the third coming of the dream, he rose and strapped his pack from long habit upon his back and took the road to Dublin. For three long weary days he traveled, barely staying his fast, and on the fourth day he came into the city.

Early in the day he found the bridge spanning the river and all the lee-long day he stood there, changing his weight from one foot to the other, shifting his pack to ease the drag of it, scanning the faces of all who passed by. But although a great tide of people swept this way, and a great tide swept that, no one stopped and spoke to him.

At the end of the day he said to himself: "I'll find me a blind alley, and like an old dog I'll lay me down in it and die." Slowly he moved off the bridge. As he passed by the Head Inn of Dublin, the door opened and out came the landlord.

To the peddler's astonishment he crossed the thoroughfare and hurried after him. He clapped a strong hand on his shoulder and cried: "Arra, man hold a minute! All day I've been watching you. All day I have seen you standing on the bridge like an old rook with rent wings. And of all the people passing from the west to the east, and of all the people passing from the east to the west, not one crossing the bridge spoke aught with you. Now I am filled with a great curiosity entirely to know what fetched you here."

Seeing hunger and weariness on the peddler, he drew him toward the inn. "Come; in return for having my curiosity satisfied you shall have rest in the kitchen yonder, with bread and cheese and ale. Come."

So the peddler rested his bones by the kitchen hearth and he ate as he hadn't eaten in many days. He was satisfied at long last and the landlord repeated his question. "Peddler, what fetched you here?"

"For three nights running I had a dream—" began the peddler, but he got no further.

The landlord of the Head Inn threw back his head and laughed. How he laughed, rocking on his feet, shaking the whole length of him!

"A dream you had, by my soul, a dream!" He spoke when he could get his breath. "I could be telling you were the cut of a man to have dreams, and to listen to them, what's more. Rags on your back and hunger in your cheeks and age upon you, and I'll wager not a farthing in your pouch. Well, God's blessing on you and your dreams."

The peddler got to his feet, saddled his pack, and made for the door. He had one foot over the sill when the landlord hurried after him and again clapped a hand on his shoulder.

"Hold, Master Peddler," he said, "I too had a dream, three nights running." He burst into laughter again, remembering it. "I dreamed there came a knocking on this very door, and the latch lifted, and, standing in the doorway, as you are standing, I saw Saint Patrick. He pointed with one finger to the road running westward and he said: 'Landlord, Landlord of the Head Inn, take *that* road to Ballaghadereen. When you come to the crossroads you will find a wee cabin, and beside the cabin a wee garden, and in the center of the garden a cherry tree. Dig deep under the tree and you will find gold—much gold.'"

The landlord paused and drew his sleeve across his mouth to hush his laughter.

"Ballaghadereen! I never heard of the place. Gold under a cherry tree—whoever heard of gold under a cherry tree! There is only one dream that I hear, waking or sleeping, and it's the dream of gold, much gold, in my own pocket. Aye, listen, 'tis a good dream." And the landlord thrust a hand into his pouch and jangled the coins loudly in the peddler's ear.

Back to Ballaghadereen went the peddler, one foot ahead of the other. How he got there I cannot be telling you. He unslung his pack, took up a mattock lying near by, and dug under the cherry tree. He dug deep and felt at last the scraping of the mattock against something hard and smooth. It took him time to uncover it and he found it to be an old sea chest, of foreign pattern and workmanship, bound around with bands of brass. These he broke, and lifting the lid he found the chest full of gold, tarnished and clotted with mold; pieces-of-six and pieces-of-eight and Spanish doubloons.

I cannot begin to tell the half of the goodness that the peddler put into the spending of that gold. But this I know. He built a chapel at the crossroads—a resting-place for all weary travelers, journeying thither.

And after he had gone the neighbors had a statue made of him and placed it facing the crossroads. And there he stands to this day, a pack on his back and a dog at his heels.

The Leprechaun; or, Fairy Shoemaker

William Allingham

Little Cowboy, what have you heard,
    Up on the lonely rath's green mound?
Only the plaintive yellow bird
    Sighing in sultry fields around,
Chary, chary, chary, chee-ee!—
Only the grasshopper and the bee?—
    "Tip tap, rip-rap,
    Tick-a-tack-too!
  Scarlet leather, sewn together,
    This will make a shoe.
  Left, right, pull it tight.
    Summer days are warm;
  Underground in winter,
    Laughing at the storm!"
Lay your ear close to the hill.
Do you not catch the tiny clamor,
Busy click of an elfin hammer,
Voice of the Leprechaun singing shrill
    As he merrily plies his trade?
    He's a span
    And a quarter in height.

Get him in sight, hold him tight,
And you're a made
Man!

You watch your cattle the summer day,
Sup on potatoes, sleep in the hay;
How would you like to roll in your carriage,
Look for a duchess's daughter in marriage?
Seize the Shoemaker—then you may!
"Big boots a-hunting,
Sandals in the hall,
White for a wedding-feast,
Pink for a ball.
This way, that way,
So we make a shoe;
Getting rich every stitch,
Tick-tack-too!"
Nine-and-ninety treasure-crocks
This keen miser-fairy hath,
Hid in mountains, woods, and rocks,
Ruin and round-tow'r, cave and rath,
And where the cormorants build;
From times of old
Guarded by him;
Each of them fill'd
Full to the brim
With gold!

I caught him at work one day, myself,
 In the castle-ditch, where foxglove grows,—
A wrinkled, wizen'd, and bearded Elf,
 Spectacles stuck on his pointed nose,
 Silver buckles to his hose,
 Leather apron—shoe in his lap—
  "Rip-rap, tip-tap,
  Tick-tack-too!
(A cricket skipp'd upon my cap!
  Away the moth flew!)
 Buskins for a fairy prince,
  Brogues for his son,—
 Pay me well, pay me well,
  When the job is done!"
The rogue was mine, beyond a doubt.
I stared at him; he stared at me;
"Servant, Sir!" "Humph!" says he,
 And pull'd a snuffbox out.
He took a long pinch, look'd better pleased,
 The queer little Leprechaun;
Offer'd the box with a whimsical grace,—
Pouf! he flung the dust in my face,
 And, while I sneezed,
 Was gone!

Earth Day and Arbor Day

OBSERVED AS PROCLAIMED IN SPRING

What was given
Me by birth
Was not heaven,
It was earth.
Though some other
House be fine,
Strange old father,
This is mine.

"Prodigal Son," by Witter Bynner

The safeguarding of the earth we share with other living things is of deep concern to us. Fresh air, clean water, clear skies, and the wealth found in our natural environment are for everyone, now and in the future. As the writer-naturalist Henry David Thoreau wrote more than a century ago, "What is the use of a house, if you haven't got a tolerable planet to put it on?"

Ecology was an unfamiliar word in Thoreau's time. But today young and old are aware of the interrelationships within our environment. People of all ages work to protect America's natural resources, our soil, minerals, water, forests, and wildlife. The goal is to improve the quality of life for all.

Two special days, one recent in origin, the other already a hundred years old, emphasize the protection of America's natural environment.

In response to efforts made by conservationists, scientists, civic leaders, teachers, and students, Earth Day was established to renew environmental awareness. It is a celebration of the world's beauty. Earth Day was first observed on April 22, 1970, but many communities have often chosen the first of spring, March 21, for local programs.

Celebration may take the form of activities. Girls and boys, for example, clean a beach, a park, or a wilderness area. They plant trees and flowers or take part in bird walks.

Reading about naturalists and sampling what they have written can suggest ideas for observing Earth Day. John James Audubon's paintings of birds and animals have preserved some of America for us. We can thank John Muir, the Scottish-born naturalist, for helping save forests and park lands. Theodore Roosevelt during his Presidency gave attention to the conservation of natural resources. Rachel Carson, a scientist, told eloquently in *Silent Spring* how chemical pollution can alter our world. And there are writers who awaken young readers to the wonders of nature—Jean George, Sterling North, Eleanor B. Heady, and Bill Perry.

The first Arbor Day was observed on April 10, 1872, in Nebraska. This special day for tree planting was the idea of J. Sterling Morton, a newspaper editor and political leader who was interested in natural history.

Today Arbor Day is celebrated in the United States and Canada, with each state or province setting the date to fit its climate. Conservation is the broad purpose behind Arbor Day. Not only are trees planted and woodlands safeguarded, but the wise use of resources is urged.

As we make Earth Day and Arbor Day living holidays, our world will be the "tolerable planet" Thoreau wanted.

Come Out and Look!

Donald Culross Peattie

Did you ever wake up early and slip out into a world fresh with a new day? The familiar scene sparkles with beauty and wonder and the sense of possible adventure. The air smells, perhaps, of pine needles and wood smoke and a secret, earthy odor like mushrooms. The grass is alight with dewdrops darting tiny rainbow fires. There may be squirrels playing tag in the trees, tweaking each other's tails, behaving as if life were one long frolic. Or crows are telegraphing in their ragged code all the gossip of the sunburnt clearings, the far-off groves. The ants in their dusty hill at your feet are toiling, the workers slavishly hurrying to and fro, the soldiers patrolling stiffly. On a branch a black and yellow spider works out in glittering silk the perfect geometry of her web. And through the aspens runs a panic whispering, as if the trees leaned together to tell old tales of Indian scares and forest dangers.

How did it all come to be here, this shining, quivering, intensely alive world of Nature? Is that only an empty cawing, or have the crows a real language? How does the spider know how to spin her complicated web? How are the ants communicating with one another? Why do the aspen leaves turn like that, with a rustle and patter and twinkle, when the breeze is too faint to stir the leaves of other trees?

Every question is a path inviting you into the adventure of the morning. As soon as you start off on such questions, you are beginning to be a naturalist. And when you begin to find out the answers, the world of Nature takes on a new dimension, as though you had put on glasses which gave depth where everything was flat before, and sharpened all to sudden clarity.

For curiosity is the beginning of natural history—which has no end. The history of Nature, the study of living things, is too vast a subject to get between the covers of a book like this. We couldn't begin to open up, let alone answer, all the questions that will occur to you just from looking at the pictures. And many questions have no answer—yet. Many common happenings are mysterious still, like the migration of birds, or the return of salmon from the sea to their breeding grounds upriver. The science of natural history is never through with its work; it is an endless journey of discovery that is taken up, and carried a little farther, by each generation. The generations come and go. The wonder and beauty of Nature remain.

This life of ours, which is shared by the crows and the squirrels, the ants and the spiders, is itself the most profound of all the mysteries. Where it began, no one can say, and where it goes to, not the wisest knows. We only feel it, warm and secret in our blood; we see it in the racing of a dog across the grass, hear it in the whistle of a bird, know it as a God-sent gift to be cared for as sacred, whether in ourselves or others. Life, like the morning light streaming down from the sun, fills the world with color and warmth and delight. It is when the tiny prism of the dewdrop catches the sunshine that we can see the rainbow tints in it. So in a book like this we can only catch glimpses of the glittering great whole of Nature.

The study of life is called biology, and much of it is done in laboratories by trained scientists. But the happy, out-of-doors side of the same study is natural history. And anyone can pursue it, and make some good catches too. Just going fishing is apt to be a lesson in natural history, and so is raising racing pigeons or making a butterfly collection or even going to the zoo. Sharp eyes, an inquiring mind, and a good memory are the only laboratory equipment you need. Young people have a finer set of such tools than the most learned oldsters.

In ornithology (the science of birds) the case is well known of an eleven-year-old girl who could name every kind of duck, as far off as she could see it, by the way it flew. Most duck hunters, grown men, will tell you that it takes years of experience to master the difficult subject of the ducks. But since no one remembered to tell this girl how hard it was, she found it quite easy. She had good eyes, close attention, and a memory that kept what it caught. And these are much more useful than the costliest binoculars ever made.

Not long ago there was a boy who went fishing, and "never got a bite." Yet he came home with the biggest bite you ever saw— the jawbone of a mastodon, an extinct kind of elephant! He had uncovered it in the bank of a stream. He drew a picture of it, explaining his find, and sent it to a natural history museum in Buffalo. The very next day brought some of the museum scientists down to his hometown. And when they uncovered the rest of the mastodon skeleton, they found it was an entirely new kind—or, as the scientists say, a new species.

Not all of us can discover a species new to science. But if a thing is new to you or me, it is as good as new. Nor can anybody ever come to the end of discovery. "The world is so full of a number of things," says the cheerful verse, "I'm sure we should all be as happy as kings."

Just what is that number—the number of living things in this world? The number of *kinds* of living things, that is, of species?

It's a good question, but not an easy one. It can't be answered exactly. Naturalists have not finished the count; they are still exploring the world, finding new species in the depths of the sea, in the tropical jungles, even right around us in the thickly settled parts of the globe. Therefore we can give only a rough estimate. It makes a grandly simple sum:

About   700,000 species of animals known
About   <u>300,000</u> species of plants known
The total is: About 1,000,000 species of known living things

One million species, each with its own name, size, shape, color, habits, range! Who could master so much knowledge? Nobody, of course, not the cleverest student in the world, not in a hundred years. No wonder that the science of natural history is carried on by specialists, who limit themselves each to his own field of interest. The older such a scientist grows, the more he knows about less and less! But you and I are free as the morning to learn only for fun. And learning is a gate that swings wide open, into the out-of-doors, where you will find yourself happy and at home in Nature for all your life long.

Tommy

Gwendolyn Brooks

I put a seed into the ground
And said, "I'll watch it grow."
I watered it and cared for it
As well as I could know.

One day I walked in my backyard,
And oh, what did I see!
My seed had popped itself right out,
Without consulting me.

APRIL

Easter

OBSERVED ON THE FIRST SUNDAY AFTER THE FIRST FULL MOON
BETWEEN MARCH 22 AND APRIL 25

Easter is the festival of spring, hope, and resurrection. The earth revives, and all around we see greening grass, flowers, budding trees, and returning birds. Winter's hold over us is broken with spring's arrival. And indeed the name "Easter" may come from Eostre, the goddess of spring who was once worshipped in northern Europe.

The religious holiday we call Easter commemorates the resurrection of Jesus Christ as it is described in the Gospels of the New Testament. It is a feast of hope, the triumph of life over death.

Many symbols and traditions belong to the Easter season. Flowers decorate homes and churches, and the white Easter lily is especially lovely. Both a lighted candle and an egg are symbols of the miracle of life. Eggs intricately decorated are part of the folk art of many middle-European countries, while the Pennsylvania Dutch have kept the custom of making Easter egg trees. Children hunt colored eggs, perhaps not knowing this is a centuries-old tradition. In the United States, some lucky children are invited to roll eggs on the White House lawn, perhaps watched by the President and his family.

Chicks, rabbits, and lambs are Easter symbols, too. In Scotland, it means good fortune to see a lamb on Easter, and in many countries children are told the Easter rabbit brings baskets of eggs. A European legend says the sun dances for joy on Easter, and the Irish awake at dawn to gather on hillsides to see the sunrise. Religious services at sunrise are shared by many worshippers here.

Whether Easter is kept for its deep Christian meaning or simply observed as a welcome to spring, it's a joyous, happy day.

April

John Updike

It's spring! Farewell
  To chills and colds!
The blushing, girlish
  World unfolds

Each flower, leaf,
  And blade of sod—
Small letters sent
  To her from God.

The sky's a herd
  Of prancing sheep,
The birds and fields
  Abandon sleep,

And jonquils, tulips,
  Daffodils
Bloom bright upon
  The wide-eyed hills.

All things renew.
  All things begin.
At church, they bring
  The lilies in.

The White Blackbird: An Easter Story

Padraic Colum

"Oh, no, it cannot be," said all the creatures of the farmyard when the little wren told them what she had seen.

"Yes, yes, yes," said the little wren excitedly, "I flew and I fluttered along the hedges, and I saw it, just as I tell you."

"What did you see, oh, what did you see?" asked the foolish pigeons. They came to where the cock with the hens were standing, and they stretched out their necks to hear what was being said.

"Something too terrible to talk to foolish creatures about," said the cock as he went gloomily away.

"Too terrible, too terrible," said the robin redbreast mournfully, as she went hopping under the hedge.

•

Inside the house the Boy was standing, and he was looking into a cage. Within that cage was a bird he had caught. It was the most wonderful of all birds, for it was a white Blackbird. Now you might live a whole lifetime and never once see a white Blackbird. But this Boy had not only seen a white Blackbird—he had caught one.

He had put the white Blackbird into a cage, and he was going to keep it forever. He was a lonely Boy, this Boy who had caught the white Blackbird. His father he had never known. His mother was dead. He lived in the house of his grandmother, his mother's mother.

His father had once lived here, but that was at a time that the Boy had no remembrance of. Then, his mother being dead, his father and his grandmother had quarreled, and after that his father went away and was never heard of afterward. The Boy had no one to take him by the hand as other boys had. He used to tell his grandmother about seeing boys walking with their fathers, the boys holding their fathers' hands. But he had given up telling her about such sights, for she looked lonely when he spoke of them.

Now the Boy had a bird for his very own. That was a joy to him. The night before the Peep-show Man had been in the house. He came out carrying a lantern. He held the lantern into a bush. The light came upon a bird that was resting there. Dazzled by the light, the bird did not move, and the Peep-show Man put his hand upon the bird, caught it, and gave it to the Boy to keep. This was the white Blackbird.

The Boy put the bird into an empty cage. Now that he had something of his own, he would not be lonely nor sorry for himself when he saw such and such a boy walking with his father on the Easter Sunday that was coming. All day he watched the strange, white bird. And that night as he sat by the fire his eyes were upon the cage, and he watched the stirring of the white Blackbird within.

•

The robin redbreast that in the winter goes along under the hedge, and the little wren that flies along the top of the hedge, were talking to each other. "Always, on Easter Sunday," said the wren, "I sing my first song of the year. My first song is for the risen Lord." "And mine, too," said the robin redbreast. "But now we will not know that it is Easter Morning and that it is time to sing for the risen Lord. For the white Blackbird always showed itself to us in times before, and when it showed itself we knew it was Easter indeed."

"O now we know what has happened," said the foolish pigeons. "The Boy has caught the white Blackbird that used to appear just before the sun was up every Easter Morning. He has brought the white Blackbird into the house and he has put it into a cage. It will not be able to show itself. Dear, dear, dear! We are truly sorry."

"The songs that the robin and the wren sing are not so very important," said the cock. "But think of the proclamation that I have made every Easter Morning. *Mok an o-ee Slaun*, 'The Son of the Virgin is safe.' I made it when the white Blackbird showed himself. Now men will not know that they may be rejoiceful."

"I—" said the wren, looking around very bravely.

"The world will be the worse for not hearing my tidings," said the cock.

"I—" said the wren again.

"The wren is trying to say something, and no one will listen to her," said robin redbreast.

"Oh, by all means let the wren keep on talking," said the cock, and he went away.

"Tell us, tell us," said the pigeons.

"I," said the little wren, "will try to set the white Blackbird free."

"How, how—" said the foolish pigeons.

"I might fly into the house when no one is watching," said the wren. "I can really slip into and out of places without being seen.

90

I might manage to open the door of the cage that the white Blackbird is in."

"Oh, it is terrible in the house," said the foolish pigeons, "we went in once, picking grains. The door was closed on us. It was dark in there. And we saw the terrible, green eyes of the cat watching us. It is terrible in the house." Then the pigeons flew away.

"I should be afraid to go in," said the robin redbreast, "now that they have mentioned the eyes of the cat."

"I *am* afraid," said the little wren. "And there is no one that would miss me if anything terrible befell me. I really am so afraid that I want to fly right away from this place."

But then, although her little heart was beating very fast, the wren flew up on the thatched porch. There was no one could see her there, so small and so brown she was. When darkness came outside she fluttered into the house. She hid in a corner of the dresser behind a little luster jug. She watched the cage that had the white Blackbird in it. She saw the door of the house closed and bolted for the night.

Oh, all in a fright and a flutter was the little brown wren as she hid in one of the houses of men. She saw the terrible cat sleeping by the hearth. She saw, when the fire burned low, how the cat rose and stretched herself and looked all around the house with her terrible eyes. The Boy and his grandmother had now gone up to bed. The wren could still see by the light that blazed up on the hearth. The cat went up one step of the stairs; but only a step. For as the wren fluttered up and alighted on the top of the cage the cat heard the sound that she made, light and all as it was, and she turned back and looked at the cage, and the little wren knew that the cat saw her and would watch her.

There was a little catch on the door of the cage. The wren pulled at it with her beak. She said to the bird within, "O white messenger—"

"How shall I fly out of the house—tell me, tell me," said the white Blackbird.

"We will fly up the chimney, and away," said the little wren as she opened the door.

•

Before the darkness had quite gone a man came along the road that went by that house. He had on the clothes of a soldier. He stood and looked at the house as he came before it. His little boy was there. But he would not stay to see him. The memory of the quarrel that he had had with the woman who lived there, the boy's grandmother, came over him. His heart was made bitter by that memory, and he would not cross her threshold.

It was near daylight now. Out of the hedge came a thin, little song. It was the song of the wren, he knew, and he smiled as he listened to it. He heard another song, a song with joyous notes in it, the first song that the robin sings from the hedge tops. All the times before she has been going under the hedges without a song.

And then he heard the cock crow. Loudly, loudly, the cock cried "Mok an o-ee Slaun, mok an o-ee Slaun," and the man remembered that this was Easter Morning. He did not go on now. He waited, and he stood looking at the house.

And then, upon the thatch of the porch he saw a strange bird— a strange, white bird. The man could not go on now. Only once in a lifetime might one see a white Blackbird. And this was the second time he had seen one. Once before, and on an Easter Morning too, he had seen a white Blackbird. He had come to this house. Some one was living in it then who was dead since. The girl who became the mother of his boy was living here. He had come for her to this house so that they might go out together and see the sun rising on Easter Morning. And when he had come before the house he had seen a strange bird on the thatch of the porch—he had seen the white Blackbird then as he saw it now.

He did not go.

Then out of the house came a little Boy. He held an empty cage in his hand. He looked all around. He saw the white Blackbird upon the porch, and he held his hands to the bird as if trying to draw it down to him again.

The man went to the Boy. And the Boy, knowing him, caught the hand that was held to him. The Boy drew the man within. There was a woman at the hearth. She turned and saw the man.

"And you are safe, my daughter's comrade?" said the woman as she drew the man to her. "And now the child will have his father to take him by the hand this Easter." The Boy felt that he would never again be lonely. He heard the robin singing. He heard the wren singing. He heard the cock outside telling the world about the risen Lord. He saw the white Blackbird flying away.

in Just-
spring

E. E. Cummings

in Just-
spring   when the world is mud-
luscious the little
lame balloonman

whistles   far   and wee

and eddieandbill come
running from marbles and
piracies and it's
spring

when the world is puddle-wonderful

the queer
old balloonman whistles
far   and   wee
and bettyandisbel come dancing

from hop-scotch and jump-rope and

it's
spring
and
      the

            goat-footed

balloonMan   whistles
far
and
wee

MAY

Mother's Day

OBSERVED ON THE SECOND SUNDAY IN MAY

Mother's Day is a family holiday celebrated in the United States, Canada, and Mexico. This special day was suggested in 1872 by Julia Ward Howe, an early leader in securing women's rights, but interest was not widespread.

It was in 1907 that Anna Jarvis took up the cause of a day to honor mothers, and she is credited with founding Mother's Day. The first observances were held at churches in 1908 in Grafton, West Virginia, and Philadelphia, both in honor of Mrs. Jarvis's mother. Her flower garden had been one of her mother's joys, and the carnation a favorite flower, thus it was natural for the carnation to become associated with this day. When President Woodrow Wilson issued the first proclamation, in 1914, making the second Sunday in May Mother's Day, he wore a white carnation, a tribute to the memory of his own mother. Flags were to be displayed, the proclamation said, "as a public expression of our love and reverence for the mothers of the country."

Mothers and foster mothers are often given little gifts of love made by their children or chosen by grown-up sons and daughters. Mothers no longer living are remembered with fondness. Once a white birch was planted on the White House grounds in honor of the mothers of the Presidents. While there may be public honors in the name of motherhood, Mother's Day is first and most importantly a family custom, a loving celebration.

The Merchant

Rabindranath Tagore

Imagine, mother, that you are to stay at home and I am to travel into strange lands.

Imagine that my boat is ready at the landing fully laden.

Now think well, mother, before you say what I shall bring for you when I come back.

Mother, do you want heaps and heaps of gold?

There, by the banks of golden streams, fields are full of golden harvest.

And in the shade of the forest path the golden *champa* flowers drop on the ground.

I will gather them all for you in many hundred baskets.

Mother, do you want pearls big as the raindrops of autumn?

I shall cross to the pearl island shore.

There in the early morning light pearls tremble on the meadow flowers, pearls drop on the grass, and pearls are scattered on the sand in spray by the wild sea-waves.

My brother shall have a pair of horses with wings to fly among the clouds.

For father I shall bring a magic pen that, without his knowing, will write of itself.

For you, mother, I must have the casket and jewel that cost seven kings their kingdoms.

The Cap
That Mother Made

A Swedish Tale

There was once a little boy called Anders. One day Anders' mother gave him a present, a cap that she herself had knit for him. It was a very pretty cap! It was red except for a little part in the middle which was green because there wasn't enough red wool to finish it all. And the tassel was blue.

Anders put the cap on his head and his mother and father told him that he looked very fine in it. Then his brothers and sisters walked around him to see how he looked from the front and the back and from each side. They, too, agreed that Anders looked very fine. So Anders put his hands in his pockets and went out for a walk, for he wanted everyone to see the lovely cap his mother had made him.

The first person he met was a farmer. The farmer was walking beside his cart which was loaded with peat, but when he saw Anders' new cap he stopped walking and made a deep bow. Anders kept right on walking and he held his head very high for he was proud to be wearing his pretty new cap.

The next person he met was Lars, the tanner's boy. Lars was

a big boy, much bigger than Anders. He was so big, in fact, that he wore high boots and carried a jackknife. But when Lars saw Anders and his splendid new cap, he stood still and looked at it and then went up close to feel it and to play with the blue tassel.

"I'll give you my jackknife if you give me your cap," he said.

Now Anders knew that as soon as one has a jackknife one is almost a man. But he couldn't give up, even for the knife, the cap his mother had made him.

"I'm sorry, Lars," he said, "but I cannot give you my cap."

And off he went down the road. At the crossroads he met a little old lady. She made a deep curtsey to Anders and said, "Little boy, you look so fine, why don't you go to the king's ball?"

"I think I will," Anders replied. "With this cap on my head I am certainly fit to visit the king."

And off he went to the king's palace. But at the gate of the palace two soldiers stopped him.

"Where are you going, little boy?" one of the soldiers asked.

"I am going to the king's ball," Anders replied.

"You cannot go to the king's ball," said the soldier. "No one can go without a uniform."

"Surely," thought Anders, "my cap is as fine as any uniform!"

But the soldiers didn't think so and Anders felt very sad. Just then the princess came to the gate of the palace. She saw the splendid red cap on Anders' head and said to the soldiers, "What is wrong? Why won't you let this little boy come to the king's ball?"

"He has no uniform," one of the soldiers told her. "No one can go without a uniform."

"His fine cap will do just as well as a uniform," the princess said. "He shall come to the ball with me."

So the princess took Anders by the hand and together they went through the gate, up the broad marble steps, down the long hall and into the ballroom. In the ballroom ladies and gentlemen wearing fine clothes of silk and satin stood about talking with one another. But when they saw Anders walking beside the princess and saw the red cap on his head, they bowed very low and they probably thought that he was a prince.

At the end of the ballroom was a long table with rows of golden plates on it and rows of golden goblets. On large silver platters there were tarts and cakes and all manner of fine things to eat and in the goblets there was red wine. The princess sat down on a golden chair at the end of the table and Anders sat down on the chair beside her.

"But you cannot eat with your cap on your head," said the princess, and she started to take it off.

"Oh, yes! I can eat just as well with it on," Anders said, and he held on to it with both his hands.

"Will you give it to me if I give you a kiss?" the princess asked.

Anders shook his head. The princess was beautiful and he would like to be kissed by her, but he would not give up the cap that Mother made.

But the princess filled his pockets full of cakes and cookies and she put her own golden necklace around his neck and then she bent down and kissed him.

"Now," she said, "will you give me the cap?"

Anders thanked her for the cakes and cookies, the necklace and the kiss, but he wouldn't take his hands from his head.

Just then the king himself entered the ballroom. He was wearing a mantle of blue velvet, bordered with ermine, and on his head was a large gold crown. When he saw Anders sitting in the golden chair, he smiled at him.

"That is a very fine cap you have," he said.

"Yes, it is," said Anders. "My mother made it for me, but everyone wants to get it away from me."

"Surely you would like to change caps with me," said the king.

He took off his large golden crown and held it out to him. With his other hand he reached for Anders' little red cap.

Anders didn't answer a word. He jumped out of his chair and dashed across the ballroom and ran down the long hall and skipped down the broad marble steps, and went out of the gate that led to the king's palace. He ran so fast that all the cakes and cookies fell out of his pocket and the golden necklace that the princess had given him fell from his neck.

But he had his cap! He had his cap! He had his cap! He held it tight with both his hands and ran home to his mother's cottage. When he got there he told his mother and his father, his brothers and his sisters all that had happened to him during the day. He told them how everyone admired his lovely red cap, but how everyone tried to get it away from him.

When he came to the part about how the king offered his golden crown for the little cap, Anders' big brother said, "You were very foolish, Anders! Think of all the things you could buy if you were king! High leather boots, a jackknife or a sword, even a cap finer than your own—one that is red all over and has a feather on it."

But Anders grew very angry and his face grew very red. "I was not foolish!" he cried. "Nowhere in the world is there a finer cap than the one my mother made me!"

And then his mother took him on her lap and kissed him.

The Flute

Wang Mou Fang,
translated by Henry H. Hart

When I had a little leisure,
I gave my son some lessons
On the flute.

Autumn has come,
And in the courtyard
The wei plants
Are flaming red.

On the wind
I hear his piping,
And my heart
Is filled with joy,
That his flute
Can bring such pleasure
To my happy little boy.

Memorial Day

Memorial Day, also called Decoration Day, is a patriotic holiday in the United States. It honors the memory of all those who have lost their lives in this nation's service during wars.

The observance of Memorial Day began during the Civil War when graves were decorated with flags and flowers. In the North, an early observance was at Waterloo, New York, and in the South, at Columbus, Mississippi. A national Memorial Day was held in 1868 when General John A. Logan ordered the Grand Army of the Republic, the organization of Union veterans of the Civil War, to hold ceremonies for their dead comrades and strew their graves with flowers. To muffled drumbeats, men in blue uniforms marched to nearby cemeteries while children ran along, carrying flowers. James Garfield, later to be President, declared at the National Cemetery in Arlington, Virginia, that "no heroic sacrifice is ever lost."

In the years that have followed, there have been Memorial Day services at Arlington, on battlefields, and at commemorative sites. In 1922, the Lincoln Memorial was dedicated in Washington, D.C., on Memorial Day.

Although this national holiday was first held to honor those who died in the Civil War, it is now a day for tribute to all who have been lost in the service of their country, wherever their graves may be. Of the dead of World War I, we still hear these lines by John McCrae,

> "In Flanders fields, the poppies blow
> Between the crosses, row on row."

Since the close of World War I, Memorial Day has also meant the observance of Poppy Day, when ex-servicemen sell artificial poppies for the benefit of disabled and needy war veterans.

"Old Abe" American Eagle

Lorraine Sherwood

The American Bald Eagle is the national bird and official emblem of the United States. It is pictured on the Great Seal, on the President's flag, and on some coins and paper money.

It was during sugar making time in the Chippewa country of Wisconsin. The Indians of the Flambeau tribe had their village on the hill overlooking Flambeau Lake, where the land was thickly wooded with sugar maples and great dark pine trees. It was, so everyone said, good country for eagles.

Apparently the birds were of this opinion, for a pair of bald eagles built their nest in a tall pine tree, safe, from human beings, or so it seemed until Chief Sky selected that particular tree to cut down. As the tall pine fell, such a squawking arose from the topmost branches that he was startled. The commotion came from a nest, a tremendous one, bigger than a wash tub. It was made of loosely woven grass and twigs, held firmly together with dried mud. In it were two indignant eaglets.

As there was no sign of the eagle parents, Chief Sky carefully gathered up the nest with its noisy occupants and carried it back to his home in the Indian village. One of the baby birds soon died, but the other, who was to become world famous, grew into a handsome young eagle.

The Indian children played with the young bird and it soon became quite tame. In the summer, Chief Sky made his yearly canoe trip to the town of Eau Claire. Usually he carried a stock of furs, moccasins and other beaded trinkets, but this year he added something more important—the eaglet! It was not every day that an Indian came into town bringing a fine young eagle.

Almost anyone could have taken a fancy to the bird, and he might have lived out his life quietly in Eau Claire. But at Jims Falls, Daniel McCann came along and offered to exchange a bushel of corn for the eaglet. Chief Sky agreed and the little fellow changed hands. A few months later the Civil War broke out, and Daniel McCann began to have ideas as to what might be a good place for an eagle.

Soldiers, he knew, often chose mascots to bring them luck. What better mascot could there possibly be than a live American eagle? So he decided to try and sell the bird to the Eighth Wisconsin Regiment.

At first the soldiers were doubtful. "Buy an eagle? We can't take a live bird into battle with us."

Just then a citizen of the town came forward saying, "Don't you realize that no finer symbol could be chosen to make victory certain?"

"That's true!" agreed the men.

Then, another civilian stepped in, bought the eagle and presented it to Company C.

With all formality, "the new recruit from Chippewa" was sworn into the Army. Solemnly the regimental doctor made a careful examination of the eagle's claws, beak and wings. Then a rosette of red-white-and blue ribbon was tied around his neck.

"I'll take care of him," volunteered James McGinnis, and so became the first eagle bearer in our nation's history.

Roman regiments had gone into battle with an eagle standard— that of an American regiment might well be a live eagle. So McGinnis made a staff with a perch that could easily be carried, and two patriotic members of the Ladies Aid Society presented a small flag for each side of it.

The soldiers led by their American Eagle on his perch beside the Stars and Stripes went to La Crosse where they were warmly welcomed, then on to Madison, the capital of Wisconsin.

The regiment stayed three days in Madison and thousands came to see the war eagle. It was decided about this time that such a famous bird should have a name, so Captain Perkins christened him "Old Abe" in honor of President Lincoln. The company, by its own vote became the "Eau Claire Eagles," but to the public the Eighth Wisconsin was always "The Eagle Regiment." The Quartermaster had an elaborate new perch made in the shape of a shield on which were painted the Stars and Stripes. Old Abe always rode to the left of the colors in battle or on march, and was carried in the same manner as the flag.

The Eagle Regiment left for Chicago, receiving ovations all along the way. It was evening when they arrived in the city, and the men formed in platoons to march through the streets. The spectators, astonished at the sight of an eagle carried at the head of his company, roared in delight, but Abe seemed to take it without turning a feather.

Abe's fame continued to spread throughout the country.

"I'll pay five hundred dollars for that bird," said one gentleman.

"I'll swap my farm for him," offered another.

"No money can buy him," was always Captain Perkins' reply.

In the middle of October the Eagle Regiment was ordered to advance toward the front. At Big River, finding the bridge had been burned, the soldiers had to take ammunition and supplies across on their backs. Tired and discouraged they silently waded through the cold water, when all at once, Abe who was leading the van of the column, suddenly burst into a cheery note. The men's spirits rose at once.

"Come on fellows, let's whistle with him."

"What a bird!"

Old Abe's company had its baptism of fire at Frederickstown on the twenty-first day of October. Apparently realizing that his comrades were facing death the Eagle gnawed at his perch and then whirled round and round like a top, screeching with excitement. Almost crazed by this new experience, Abe did not quiet down until the fierce fighting ended and their first victory was won.

By the time the company went into winter quarters at Sulphur Springs, Abe had become an experienced soldier. Tales of his antics relieved the long homesick hours, and at night the men would gather around the campfire and swap stories of his latest pranks.

"Did you see Abe get away with a chicken today? Swiped it right under the cook's nose, slick as a whistle."

"Abe marched into my tent again and tore another of my shirts to shreds!"

"That eagle sure knows military tactics. When he hears the call to 'attention' Old Abe answers right away, and with one eye on the commander, stands with his head held straight to the front. I almost expect to see him salute."

In the spring the Eagle Regiment moved on to New Madrid. There Old Abe played among the cannon and shell and helped chase the retreating men, as his side captured six thousand prisoners. This siege was followed by a series of important victories.

With the Confederates scattered, the Eagle Regiment went into summer quarters near Clear Creek. Abe's fame grew daily, and people came from all over to see the "Yankee Eagle."

Old Abe led a charmed life, for in the fiercest fights, although always a conspicuous target, he and his bearers dodged death. Together they came through thirty-six battles and as many skirmishes, but not without making some miraculous escapes. One of the narrowest was when the Confederates tried to charge up a hill overlooking the town of Corinth, held by the Union forces. In the regimental advance were the Eagles, with Old Abe. Word had gone out that he was to be the prize.

"I would rather capture or kill that eagle than take a whole brigade," General Price had been heard to declare.

During a lull in the fighting Old Abe was exposed in plain sight.

"There he is—the eagle—capture him, boys!" commanded a Confederate officer. Immediately they opened artillery fire. The eagle watching every move, gave a note of alarm as the two armies clashed. During the confusion that followed, Abe sprang up, and circled away in the smoke, followed by a hail of bullets. For an instant he wavered as though hit. Then righted himself, wheeled around and flew back to his own lines where he was safely caught by his bearer. The battle ended next day in a victory for his side but at the cost of many lives. One of Abe's wings had been grazed by a bullet!

At last a meeting took place between Grant and Pemberton to settle the terms of the surrender of Vicksburg, and on the Fourth of July, the victorious Federal Army entered the city, with Abe riding triumphantly on his post of duty.

But the war was not yet over, and another terrible year dragged by. The battle-scarred veterans of the Eagle Regiment and their soldier bird went home on a thirty-day furlough. Everyone in Eau Claire turned out to give a rousing welcome to Old Abe and the remnants of Company C as they marched into town beside their torn battle flags. There was a great feast, followed by a reception in honor of the eagle. Seated on his perch beneath an oak tree in a beautiful garden, Abe received his old friends with dignity.

During these war years Old Abe had changed in appearance. His brown head feathers gradually turned white, and his tail feathers developed white tips. Now he was a full-grown American Bald Eagle.

Old Abe had one more battle to win at Hurricane Creek, Louisiana. The front was left open for a charge by the Eagles, and Old Abe charged with them. Above the smoke and rumble of cannon was heard his victorious scream, putting the final touch on his perpetual conquests.

Now some of Company C had served three years and were to be mustered out. Twenty-six of the original regiment and their eagle headed north, arriving at Madison in September. Crowned with honors, the fearless Eagle veteran was going home.

After his comrades returned to civilian life, the great question arose: "What shall we do with Old Abe?"

Finally the veterans decided the best thing was to present him to the State of Wisconsin.

During the presentation to the Governor, Captain Wolfe explained: "You have no idea how much the regiment thinks of this bird. He has been one of us for three years. Old Abe has always been a good soldier, he never flinched on long marches or under fire. He cheered and encouraged the men when they were low. He kept them amused at camp, and in battle he spurred them on to victory by his grit. We can never forget our American Eagle."

Once the living symbol of our country, today Old Abe is only a memory. But somehow, whenever we see our national emblem, it seems to those of us who know his story, to be more than just another eagle. It is the soldier bird from the evergreen forests of the great West who led his men in the Civil War—immortal Old Abe, the American Eagle.

JUNE

Flag Day

OBSERVED ON JUNE 14

When we sing "The Star-Spangled Banner" and recite the Pledge of Allegiance we honor the Stars and Stripes, the flag of the United States. The flag is the symbol of our land, its people, history, government, and the ideals of liberty, justice, and equality for all.

The flag with its stars and stripes is older than the Constitution of the United States. On June 14, 1777, almost a year after the American colonies had declared independence from Great Britain, the Continental Congress in Philadelphia adopted an official flag. The resolution said the flag should "be thirteen stripes alternate red and white, and the Union be thirteen stars white in a blue field representing a new constellation."

When two new states, Vermont and Kentucky, joined the Union two stars and two stripes were added to the flag. But as other states were admitted, there was a question of how the flag should be changed. The Flag Act passed by Congress on April 4, 1818, permanently set the number of stripes at thirteen to represent the thirteen original states, and provided that on the admission of each new state, one star should be added. When Alaska in 1959 and Hawaii in 1960 became states, the flag was given fifty stars.

Among famous flags is the now-tattered, huge flag that flew above Fort McHenry in the War of 1812 and inspired Francis Scott Key to write "The Star-Spangled Banner." Explorers have carried the flag with them, and Admiral Robert E. Peary planted the flag at the North Pole in 1909. An unforgettable picture from World War II was of Marines raising the flag during battle on the Pacific island of Iwo Jima. Millions watched on television as Astronauts Neil Armstrong and Edwin Aldrin on July 20, 1969, saluted the flag they had placed on the moon.

112

Not of
School Age

Robert Frost

Around bend after bend,
It was blown woods and no end.
I came to but one house,
I made but the one friend.

At the one house a child was out
Who drew back at first in doubt,
But spoke to me in a gale
That blew so he had to shout.

His cheek smeared with apple sand,
A part apple in his hand,
He pointed on up the road
As one having war-command.

A parent, his gentler one,
Looked forth on her small son
And wondered with me there
What now was being done.

His accent was not good.
But I slowly understood.
Something where I could go—
He couldn't but I could.

He was too young to go,
Not over four or so.
Well, would I please go to school,
And the big flag they had—you know

The big flag, the red-white-
And blue flag, the great sight—
He bet it was out today,
And would I see if he was right?

Benny's Flag

Phyllis Krasilovsky

The state flag of Alaska has seven gold stars that form the Big Dipper on a field of blue. An eighth star in the corner is the North Star. The flag was designed by a thirteen-year-old Alaskan schoolboy, Benjamin Benson, and adopted in 1927.

Benny was an Indian boy who lived in Alaska many years before it became a state. He had straight black hair and bright black eyes, but best of all he had the whitest white teeth and a happy, friendly smile. Everyone liked Benny, for Benny liked everyone. He had no father and mother, but he had many, many friends in the mission home where he lived. That was a place for boys and girls who had no families.

The children ate together in a big dining room. They slept in big rooms, called dormitories, which had many beds in them. And in the winter they all went to the same school that the other children in the village attended.

Benny was happy in the mission home. But sometimes before he went to sleep at night, he would gaze at the stars outside his dormitory window and long for the day when he would be a grown-up man. For then he was going to be a fine fisherman. He would use a big net like the Big Dipper to catch splendid silver fish. And like the Big Dipper, which was really a great strong bear of night, he would be big and strong himself. The North Star would guide his boat, for the North Star is the star of Alaska, the northernmost state in America.

Sometimes, when the sky was scattered with hundreds of stars, it reminded Benny of a field of forget-me-nots, the little star-shaped flowers which grow wild everywhere. The blue sky was a roof that covered Benny's Alaska at night.

In the summertime, when only the mountaintops were still covered with snow, Benny enjoyed himself on picnics with the other mission children. Sometimes he went swimming, too, though the water was often cold.

One lucky day a kind fisherman took Benny fishing with him in his boat. Almost at once Benny caught a big silver salmon all by himself. It was so big that there was enough for everyone at the mission house to eat for supper, and everyone said it was delicious.

Benny was so happy he could hardly sleep that night. He lay awake looking at the stars, dreaming his dream of becoming a real fisherman. The Big Dipper looked more like a great strong bear than ever because Benny felt so big and strong himself!

When fall came, school started again just as it does for children everywhere. But then the winter came quickly, far more quickly than it does anywhere else. The first snowy day Benny went to school wearing a parka, which is a fur-hooded jacket, and mukluks, which are fur-lined boots, and thick mittens to keep his fingers warm. He looked more like a furry bear than an Indian boy!

As he walked along the snow-covered road he wondered if all the little blue forget-me-not flowers which covered the fields in summer were now growing under the earth. In the cold winter sunshine the world was all white-and-twinkly snow. The silver fish had gone downstream to warmer places; and the fishing boats, anchored near the beach, looked like a fleet of ghost ships.

That day in school the teacher told the children that there was a contest to make a flag for Alaska. With all his heart Benny wanted to win the contest. He thought how grand it would be to see his flag carried in a parade or hung on the mission-house flagpole on holidays or flying at the masts of big ships that came to the village in the summertime. He thought how especially grand it would be to see his flag flying on the fishing boat he would have one day.

That night the boys and girls at the mission house collected crayons, paints, and paper, and made many, many designs for the flag. They sat around a big table and as they worked they talked and laughed and sometimes held up their designs for the others to see. But Benny sat quietly, thinking and thinking. For once no one could see his white teeth and happy, friendly smile. He was thinking of what he loved the most about Alaska.

Some of the children drew pictures of the beautiful snow-covered mountains in Alaska. Some drew pictures of the big fish that can be caught in Alaska. Some drew pictures of the northern lights that sometimes cross Alaskan skies.

Some drew pictures of the Alaskan forests. Some drew pictures of the Alaskan glaciers, and some drew pictures of the Alaskan rivers. And some drew star designs or stripe designs or plaid designs or flower designs.

Suddenly Benny knew what he wanted his flag to be like. He wanted his flag to be like the stars he dreamed by—gold stars spread out like the Big Dipper in the blue sky. So that is what he painted. And underneath it he wrote: "The blue field is for the Alaska sky and the forget-me-not, an Alaskan flower. The North Star is for the future state of Alaska, the most northerly of the Union. The dipper is for the Great Bear—symbolizing strength."

Benny didn't show his paper to anyone. He was too shy. He

thought the other children's designs were much better than his. Still, the next day he gave his paper to the teacher when she collected the others.

A month went by and the teacher didn't mention the contest again. Benny ice-skated and had snowball fights and went sleigh-riding with the other children. And so the winter went quickly by.

And suddenly the snow and ice began to melt. Benny no longer wore his parka and mukluks and mittens. He began to watch for the forget-me-nots in the drying fields as he walked to school.

He watched the fishermen mend their nets for the coming fishing season. He watched the world change from white to green.

Then, one day, when school was almost over, the teacher called the children together. "Children," she said, "the flag contest is ended. From all over Alaska boys and girls sent in designs for the flag. From northern Nome to the busy cities of Anchorage and Fairbanks, from the fishing towns of Seward and Petersburg, to Juneau, the capital, and the lumber town of Ketchikan . . . from everywhere came hundreds of designs. And . . . Boys and girls! *Benny's* design won the contest! From now on *Benny's* design will be Alaska's flag!"

What a proud and happy boy Benny was! And what an especially proud and happy boy he was on the Fourth of July. For on that day there was a big parade in the village to celebrate the holiday. Everyone came to see the parade—to see the marchers with their drums and fifes, to see the bright uniforms, to see the baton twirlers, to see the banners. . . . But the very first thing they saw was *BENNY.* . . . Benny marching at the head of the parade, carrying the flag he had made for the fishing boat he would have, carrying the flag he had made for Alaska!

This is a true story!

Father's Day

June is the month of graduations and roses, and it is also the month in which we honor fathers. Father's Day is popularly celebrated in the United States and Canada with special greetings and programs. A family picnic may be the order of the day.

The idea for a Father's Day was suggested by Mrs. John Bruce Dodd, who felt that men like her own father deserved a day of recognition and gratitude. She was aided by others from her home city of Spokane, Washington, and the first celebration was there in June of 1910.

Interest in honoring fathers grew, and other cities and states promoted the idea. President Woodrow Wilson proclaimed Father's Day as a holiday in 1916, two years after declaring a similar holiday in honor of mothers. Father's Day, however, did not become an annual observance until 1924, and it was only in 1972 that it became a permanently established holiday.

Like Mother's Day, Father's Day is a happy family occasion, a time to show love, pride, and admiration. Sometimes it is pleasant to turn to a book such as Theodore Roosevelt's *Letters to His Children* to glimpse the warm, deep relationships fathers and their children share.

119

A Pavane for the Nursery

William Jay Smith

Now touch the air softly,
Step gently. One, two...
I'll love you till roses
Are robin's-egg blue;
I'll love you till gravel
Is eaten for bread,
And lemons are orange,
And lavender's red.

Now touch the air softly,
Swing gently the broom.
I'll love you till windows
Are all of a room;
And the table is laid,
And the table is bare,
And the ceiling reposes
On bottomless air.

I'll love you till Heaven
Rips the stars from his coat,
And the Moon rows away in
A glass-bottomed boat;
And Orion steps down
Like a diver below,
And Earth is ablaze,
And Ocean aglow.

So touch the air softly,
And swing the broom high.
We will dust the gray mountains,
And sweep the blue sky;
And I'll love you as long
As the furrow the plow,
As However is Ever,
And Ever is Now.

the drum

Nikki Giovanni

daddy says the world is
a drum tight and hard
and i told him
i'm gonna beat
out my own rhythm

A Boy and His Pa

Marjorie Kinnan Rawlings

Home for Jody Baxter is the scrub pine country of Florida, and the story of how he grows up there is told in The Yearling. *The book is regional, but Jody and his father, Penny Baxter, have universal appeal.*

Jody looked at the sky. He could not tell the time of day in the grayness, nor how long he may have slept. He bounded up the west bank, where open gallberry flats spread without obstructions. As he stood, hesitant whether to go or stay, the rain ended as gently as it had begun. A light breeze stirred from the southwest. The sun came out. The clouds rolled together into great white billowing feather bolsters, and across the east a rainbow arched, so lovely and so various that Jody thought he would burst with looking at it. The earth was pale green, the air itself was all but visible, golden with the rain-washed sunlight, and all the trees and grass and bushes glittered, varnished with the raindrops.

122

A spring of delight boiled up within him as irresistibly as the spring of the branch. He lifted his arms and held them straight from his shoulders like a water turkey's wings. He began to whirl around in his tracks. He whirled faster and faster until his ecstasy was a whirlpool, and when he thought he would explode with it, he became dizzy and closed his eyes and dropped to the ground and lay flat in the broom sage. The earth whirled under him and with him. He opened his eyes and the blue April sky and the cotton clouds whirled over him. Boy and earth and trees and sky spun together. The whirling stopped, his head cleared and he got to his feet. He was light-headed and giddy, but something in him was relieved, and the April day could be borne again, like any ordinary day.

He turned and galloped toward home. He drew deep breaths of the pines, aromatic with wetness. The loose sand that had pulled at his feet was firmed by the rain. The return was comfortable going. The sun was not far from its setting when the longleaf pines around the Baxter clearing came into sight. They stood tall and dark against the red-gold west. He heard the chickens clucking and quarreling and knew they had just been fed. He turned into the clearing. The weathered gray of the split-rail fence was luminous in the rich spring light. Smoke curled thickly from the stick-and-clay chimney. Supper would be ready on the hearth and hot bread baking in the Dutch oven. He hoped his father had not returned from Grahamsville. It came to him for the first time that perhaps he should not have left the place while his father was away. If his mother had needed wood, she would be angry. Even his father would shake his head and say, "Son—" He heard old Caesar snort and knew his father was ahead of him.

The clearing was in a pleasant clatter. The horse whinnied at

123

the gate, the calf bleated in its stall and the milch cow answered, the chickens scratched and cackled and the dogs barked with the coming of food and evening. It was good to be hungry and to be fed and the stock was eager with an expectant certainty. The end of winter had been meager: corn short, and hay, and dried cowpeas. But now in April the pastures were green and succulent and even the chickens savored the sprouts of young grass. The dogs had found a nest of young rabbits that evening, and after such tidbits the scraps from the Baxter supper table were a matter of some indifference. Jody saw old Julia lying under the wagon, worn out from her miles of trotting. He swung open the front paling gate and went to find his father.

Penny Baxter was at the woodpile. He still wore the coat of the broadcloth suit that he had been married in, that he now wore as badge of his gentility when he went to church, or off trading. The sleeves were too short, not because Penny had grown, but because the years of hanging through the summer dampness, and being pressed with the smoothing iron and pressed again, had somehow shrunk the fabric. Jody saw his father's hands, big for the rest of him, close around a bundle of wood. He was doing Jody's work, and in his good coat. Jody ran to him.

"I'll git it, Pa."

He hoped his willingness, now, would cover his delinquency. His father straightened his back.

"I near about give you out, son," he said.

"I went to the Glen."

"Hit were a mighty purty day to go," Penny said. "Or to go anywhere. How come you to take out such a fur piece?"

It was as hard to remember why he had gone as though it had

been a year ago. He had to think back to the moment when he had laid down his hoe.

"Oh." He had it now. "I aimed to foller the honeybees and find a bee tree."

"You find it?"

Jody stared blankly.

"Dogged if I ain't forgot 'til now to look for it."

He felt as foolish as a bird dog caught chasing field mice. He looked at his father sheepishly. His father's pale blue eyes were twinkling.

"Tell the truth, Jody," he said, "and shame the devil. Wa'n't the bee tree a fine excuse to go a-ramblin'?"

Jody grinned.

"The notion takened me," he admitted, "afore I studied on the the bee tree."

"That's what I figgered. How come me to know, was when I was drivin' along to Grahamsville, I said to myself, 'There's Jody now, and the hoein' ain't goin' to take him too long. What would I do this fine spring day, was I a boy?' And then I thought, 'I'd go a-ramblin'.' Most anywhere, long as it kivered the ground."

A warmth filled the boy that was not the low golden sun. He nodded.

"That's the way I figgered," he said.

"But your Ma, now," Penny jerked his head toward the house, "don't hold with ramblin'. Most womenfolks cain't see for their lives, how a man loves so to ramble. I never let on you wasn't here. She said, 'Where's Jody?' and I said, 'Oh, I reckon he's around some'eres.'"

He winked one eye and Jody winked back.

"Menfolks has got to stick together in the name o' peace. You carry your Ma a good bait o' wood now."

Jody filled his arms and hurried to the house. His mother was kneeling at the hearth. The spiced smells that came to his nose made him weak with hunger.

"That ain't sweet 'tater pone, is it, Ma?"

"Hit's sweet 'tater pone, and don't you fellers be too long a time now, piddlin' around and visitin'. Supper's done and ready."

He dumped the wood in the box and scurried to the lot. His father was milking Trixie.

"Ma says to git done and come on," he reported. "Must I feed old Caesar?"

"I done fed him, son, sich as I had to give the pore feller." He stood up from the three-legged milking stool. "Carry in the milk and don't trip and waste it outen the gourd like you done yestiddy. Easy, Trixie—"

He moved aside from the cow and went to the stall in the shed, where her calf was tethered.

"Here, Trixie. Soo, gal—"

The cow lowed and came to her calf.

"Easy, there. You greedy as Jody."

He stroked the pair and followed the boy to the house. They washed in turn at the water-shelf and dried their hands and faces on the roller towel hanging outside the kitchen door. Ma Baxter sat at the table waiting for them, helping their plates. Her bulky frame filled the end of the long narrow table. Jody and his father sat down on either side of her. It seemed natural to both of them that she should preside.

"You-all hongry tonight?" she asked.

"I kin hold a barrel o' meat and a bushel o' biscuit," Jody said.

"That's what you say. Your eyes is bigger'n your belly."

"I'd about say the same," Penny said, "if I hadn't learned better. Goin' to Grahamsville allus do make me hongry."

"You git a snort o' 'shine there, is the reason," she said.

"A mighty small one today. Jim Turnbuckle treated."

"Then you shore didn't git enough to hurt you."

Jody heard nothing; saw nothing but his plate. He had never been so hungry in his life, and after a lean winter and slow spring, with food not much more plentiful for the Baxters than for their stock, his mother had cooked a supper good enough for the preacher. There were poke greens with bits of white bacon buried in them; sand-buggers made of potato and onion and the cooter he had found crawling yesterday; sour orange biscuits and at his mother's elbow the sweet potato pone. He was torn between his desire for more biscuits and another sand-bugger and the knowledge, born of painful experience, that if he ate them, he would suddenly have no room for pone. The choice was plain.

"Ma," he said, "kin I have my pone right now?"

She was at a pause in the feeding of her own large frame. She cut him, dexterously, a generous portion. He plunged into its spiced and savory goodness.

"The time it takened me," she complained, "to make that pone —and you destroyin' it before I git my breath—"

"I'm eatin' it quick," he admitted, "but I'll remember it a long time."

Supper was done with. Jody was replete. Even his father, who usually ate like a sparrow, had taken a second helping.

"I'm full, thank the Lord," he said.

Ma Baxter sighed.

"If a feller'd light me a candle," she said, "I'd git shut o' the dishwashin' and mebbe have time to set and enjoy myself."

Jody left his seat and lit a tallow candle. As the yellow flame wavered, he looked out of the east window. The full moon was rising.

"A pity to waste light, ain't it," his father said, "and the full moon shinin'."

He came to the window and they watched it together.

"Son, what do it put in your head? Do you mind what we said we'd do, full moon in April?"

"I disremember."

Somehow, the seasons always took him unawares. It must be necessary to be as old as his father to keep them in the mind and memory, to remember moon-time from one year's end to another.

"You ain't forgot what I told you? I'll swear, Jody. Why, boy, the bears comes outen their winter beds on the full moon in April."

"Old Slewfoot! You said we'd lay for him when he come out!"

"That's it."

"You said we'd go where we seed his tracks comin' and goin' and crisscrossin', and likely find his bed, and him, too, comin' out in April."

"And fat. Fat and lazy. The meat so sweet, from him layin' up."

"And him mebbe easier to ketch, not woke up good."

"That's it."

"When kin we go, Pa?"

"Soon as we git the hoein' done. And see bear-sign."

"Which-a-way will we begin huntin' him?"

"We'd best to go by the Glen springs and see has he come out and watered there."

"A big ol' doe watered there today," Jody said. "Whilst I was asleep. I built me a fluttermill, Pa. It run fine."

Ma Baxter stopped the clatter of her pots and pans.

"You sly scaper," she said. "That's the first I knowed you been off. You gittin' slick as a clay road in the rain."

He shouted with laughter.

"I fooled you, Ma. Say it, Ma, I got to fool you oncet."

"You fooled me. And me standin' over the fire makin' potato pone—"

She was not truly angry.

"Now, Ma," he cajoled her, "suppose I was a varmint and didn't eat nothin' but roots and grass."

"I'd not have nothin' then to rile me," she said.

At the same time he saw her mouth twist. She tried to straighten it and could not.

"Ma's a-laughin'! Ma's a-laughin'! You ain't riled when you laugh!"

He darted behind her and untied her apron strings. The apron slipped to the floor. She turned her bulk quickly and boxed his ears, but the blows were featherlight and playful. The same delirium came over him again that he had felt in the afternoon. He began to whirl around and around as he had done in the broom sage.

"You knock them plates offen the table," she said, "and you'll see who's riled."

"I cain't he'p it. I'm dizzy."

"You're addled," she said. "Jest plain addled."

It was true. He was addled with April. He was dizzy with Spring. He was as drunk as Lem Forrester on a Saturday night. His head was swimming with the strong brew made up of the sun and the air and the thin gray rain. The fluttermill had made him drunk, and the doe's coming, and his father's hiding his absence, and his mother's making him a pone and laughing at him. He was stabbed with the candlelight inside the safe comfort of the cabin; with the moonlight around it. He pictured old Slewfoot, the great black outlaw bear with one toe missing, rearing up in his winter bed and tasting the soft air and smelling the moonlight, as he, Jody, smelled and tasted them. He went to bed in a fever and could not sleep. A mark was on him from the day's delight, so that all his life, when April was a thin green and the flavor of rain was on his tongue, an old wound would throb and a nostalgia would fill him for something he could not quite remember. A whippoorwill called across the bright night, and suddenly he was asleep.

JULY

Dominion Day

Dominion Day is the birthday of Canada, celebrated with parades, fireworks, and the red-and-white maple leaf flag flying over every school and public building.

Until July 1, 1867, it seemed that there might be two countries sharing the huge land to the north of the United States. The idea of bringing the British North American Colonies under one government was not easily made a reality. Men of vision known as the Fathers of Confederation worked to unite Quebec, Ontario, Nova Scotia, and New Brunswick into the Dominion of Canada, a self-governing nation, but a member of the British Commonwealth of Nations. The men who accomplished this were John A. Macdonald, who became the first Prime Minister, Georges Étienne Cartier, Alexander Galt, George Brown, Leonard Tilley, Charles Tupper, and Thomas D'Arcy McGee.

Today Canada has ten provinces and two territories. English and French are the official languages, and the maple leaf is the national emblem.

Canada and the United States are neighbors who share many traditions. Each has known pioneer and prairie days as new settlers moved west. Friends visit back and forth across the long border, sharing sports, books, art, music, and the theater. Many of the same holidays are celebrated, and it is a pleasant coincidence that Canada and the United States have their greatest national holidays—Dominion Day and Independence Day—in the same month, July.

Once Upon
a Great Holiday

Anne Wilkinson

I remember or remember hearing
Stories that began
"Once upon a great holiday
Everyone with legs to run
Raced to the sea, rejoicing."

It may have been harvest Sunday
Or the first Monday in July
Or rockets rising for young Albert's queen.
Nobody knows. But the postman says
It was only one of those fly-by-days
That never come back again.

133

My brother counted twenty suns
And a swarm of stars in the east,
A cousin swears the west was full of moons;
My father whistled and my mother sang
And my father carried my sister
Down to the sea in his arms.

So one sleep every year I dream
The end of Ramadan
Or some high holy day
When fathers whistle and mothers sing
And every child is fair of face

And sticks and stones are loving and giving
And sun and moon embrace.

A unicorn runs on this fly-by-day,
Whiter than milk on the grass, so white is he.

A Dominion Day to Remember

Leslie McFarlane

It is 1887, and David Graham and his sister Janet are at the Great Picnic on the first of July, celebrating Canada's birthday. The festive mood of band music, the abundance of food on picnic tables, and the excitement of a balloon ascension are broken by a storm. Rain drenched, Janet skipped dangerously near when a carriage passed. Here is the adventure that follows.

The rain was over. The thunder had muttered and mumbled itself out, and birds were beginning to utter tentative cheeps and twitters in the garden, where water dripped from the leaves. A shaft of sunshine made its appearance, slanting through the kitchen window.

David, in a pair of dry overalls and a clean shirt, wriggled his toes inside a pair of woolen slippers. Janet was curled up in the rocking chair in a cotton dress much too large for her, but which made her feel grown up. Their own clothes, hung on a cord over the kitchen stove, had stopped dripping and steaming and were almost dry. The doctor, after pronouncing Janet "sound in wind and limb," had vanished as noiselessly as he had arrived.

"And don't you worry about your Uncle Ogden," said Mrs. Webster as she sat knitting by the window. "Just as soon as your clothes are dry, the coachman will fetch you back to the picnic.

Although I doubt if there'll be much going on now," she sighed. The needles flashed. "Poor Mr. Chadwick!"

"Who is Mr. Chadwick, ma'am?" inquired David.

Mrs. Webster sat up very straight, adjusted her spectacles and stared at him over the rims.

"Why, the Honorable Mr. *Albert* Chadwick," she said, as if that explained everything. "He used to be a member of Parliament."

The needles flashed again. "But he had to retire." She looked up at them. "He has been very ill, you see. Very ill. In fact..." Mrs. Webster put down the knitting needles, removed her spectacles, dabbed at her eyes with a kerchief, breathed upon the spectacles, polished them with her apron, and restored them to the bridge of her nose. "That's why he wanted it to be the greatest First of July picnic we ever had." She took off her spectacles again, and David saw that tears were streaming down her cheeks. "Why did it have to go and rain?" she said sadly.

She dried her eyes with the apron. When she spoke again her voice trembled. "Because there won't be any more First of Julys for Mr. Chadwick."

The maid, Tina, came hurrying into the kitchen.

"The children, ma'am," she gasped, stammering with excitement. "Sir John. He asked specially. He wants them fetched in."

"Oh dear!" Mrs. Webster dropped her knitting and jumped to her feet. "But they aren't presentable. Their clothes aren't dry."

"He knows that. He says they're to come as they are."

Tina seized a hairbrush from a rack over the kitchen sink and launched herself at David. As for Mrs. Webster, she ran about in small circles as if trying to decide what to do, uttering cries of distraction, until her eyes fell upon a comb. She seized it, and attacked

Janet's hair. "Get me a ribbon. Get me a ribbon. She can't go in there without a ribbon."

Tina, in the meantime, brushed David's hair until his scalp ached, combed it, tucked in his shirt, and made use of a large safety pin to reduce the slack in his overalls, all the time breathing heavily in his ear, muttering, "Oh Lordy, Lordy, and here you are without even your own clothes, and not a stitch but what we could dig out of the trunk, and going to meet John A. himself. What will your mother think when she hears? She'll be so mortified she'll die, so she will."

Then Mrs. Webster seized him, turned him around, turned up the cuffs of the overalls, and dabbed at his face with a wet washrag. While this was going on she adjured him to be polite, to say please and thank you, to remember his manners, and above all things to speak only when spoken to.

All of this David endured with patience because he had been through it all before, at home, whenever the minister called, and he realized that this performance was not peculiar to his mother but to all women whenever small boys and distinguished visitors were concerned. But there was one thing he had to know.

"Please, ma'am," he said, as Mrs. Webster straightened up and turned him around for a final inspection.

"Oh now, you're not going to tell me you have to..."

He shook his head.

"The gentleman they call Sir John. I don't know his last name."

Mrs. Webster looked incredulously at Tina. As for Tina, her mouth flew open. Then she screamed, "He doesn't *know!*"

"Don't tell me!" said Mrs. Webster, in a voice of utter amazement. "Don't *tell* me!" She put her hands on her hips. "Grown-up people!" she exclaimed. "We're all alike. Every one of us. We expect children to know everything."

"But they drove up with him in the carriage," cried Tina.

"Of course. But nobody thought to explain."

Mrs. Webster crouched in front of the children. "Listen carefully," she said in a quiet voice. "Have you ever heard of Sir John A. Macdonald?"

Janet shook her head vigorously. David nodded.

"We took him up in school," he said, trying to remember what it was they had taken up.

"Then you know that he is the Prime Minister of this country. But he is even more than that. He is one of the men who founded this nation, who brought it together. More than anyone else, he did that. So he is a very important man. When you go in there, you must pay very special attention to everything he says."

"Why?" asked Janet.

"Because years from now you will want to remember every moment, so that you can tell your children and your grandchildren all about it. You see, most of us never meet anyone really important and great in our whole lives. Not close, that is, and to talk to."

She stood up straight.

"All right, Tina. You may fetch them into the parlor."

All the way down the silent, carpeted hall Tina kept making last-minute adjustments and whispering reminders about their manners. When they reached an archway that opened on the parlor she announced in a shaky voice, "Here are the children, sir," and hastily retreated, leaving them on their own.

The parlor was a long, bright room flooded with sunshine that filtered through the lace curtains of high windows overlooking the

138

garden. By the white fireplace at the end of the room stood Sir John, one elbow on the mantel and a thumb hooked in the pocket of his waistcoat. Lying on a sofa nearby, propped up by pillows, was the Honorable Mr. Chadwick, very frail, very old, with silvery hair and skin like wax.

"Come in, youngsters. Come in." A thin, graceful hand beckoned. Janet took a firm grip on the back of David's overalls as they walked shyly over to Mr. Chadwick. His handshake was gentle, his voice kind. "Tilkerson tells me you are Tom Graham's children. I know your father. He's a fine man." He looked over at Sir John. "I believe you have already met these young people."

Sir John walked over from the fireplace.

"Very informally. I'm afraid we were all too greatly occupied for introductions," he smiled. He bowed to Janet as courteously as if she were a grown-up lady, and extended his hand. "Miss Janet."

David was sure that Janet would hide behind him in panic, but she surprised him. She held out her hand with great composure and even made a little curtsy.

"How do you do, sir," she whispered. He was proud of her.

"David." Sir John's handclasp was firm. David recalled what Mrs. Webster had told him. He must remember every moment. When Miss Flegg, his school teacher, had spoken of Sir John A. Macdonald she had called him a statesman, but somehow David had never realized that a statesman could be a living person. Sir John A. Macdonald had been merely a name like Alfred the Great or the Duke of Wellington, someone who had lived a long time ago —a remote being, shrouded in history. And here he was actually shaking hands with one of these great men.

"You traveled a long way to the picnic, they tell me," said Sir

John. David noticed his watch fob and chain, the wide lapels of his coat, the high linen collar, the rich silk cravat, the little network of veins in his big nose, the shrewd, deep-set eyes hooded by the shaggy brows. "I hope it hasn't been a great disappointment."

"We wanted to see the balloon go up," said Janet.

"Ah, yes. Professor Fitzpatrick." He turned to the Honorable Mr. Chadwick. "That must have cost you a tidy packet of money, Chad."

"My last picnic, John. I wanted it to be a big one. Something they'd remember. And I couldn't promise them a Prime Minister, although I knew you would try."

Sir John smiled.

"We didn't need balloonists in 'seventy-six, did we?"

"No, that we didn't." Old Mr. Chadwick sat up along the pillows; his eyes had a new light in them. He looked at Janet. "You weren't born then, my dear." To David he said, "And you would be a very small lad. We had great picnics, then — the greatest we've ever seen or ever will see."

"We'll never know their like again." Sir John locked his hands behind his back and paced slowly across the rug. Then he stopped and looked down at the children. "You may find this very dull," he said abruptly, "but you're not too young to understand. You see, I was the first Prime Minister of this country."

"I know, sir," said David.

"I'll always be very proud of that. But then they turned me out, and I've never been proud of that at all. I was heartsick, I tell you. And I thought and I thought and I said to myself, 'How can I reach the people? How can I tell them what I want them to know? How can I convince them that they've made a mistake, that I'm not the dreadful man my enemies tell them I am; how can I persuade them to send me back to do the work I began?'"

He paced again, his head down as if absorbed in thought. Then he looked up.

"The First of July was a great holiday by that time. Dominion Day. The first big holiday of the Canadian summer. All over the country people celebrated, and in the little towns and villages they enjoyed going out of doors and having picnics." He raised a forefinger and said, "Ah!" as if an idea had just struck him. "So I went to their picnics and talked to them there."

"And *what* picnics!" exclaimed Mr. Chadwick.

"I remember Dominion Day of 'seventy-six in the town of Uxbridge," said Sir John. There was a faraway look in his eyes as if he could see again that gathering of eleven years ago. "They walked, they came by farm wagons and buggies and democrats and carriages, and they came by train. Five thousand people. I spoke to five thousand people that summer day."

"And then there were more picnics," mused old Mr. Chadwick. "And more people."

"Ten thousand at Orangeville. Fifteen thousand at Belleville. You see, I'd been away from them too long. Up there in Ottawa all those years they didn't see me, didn't hear me, didn't know me. A nation isn't a government, it isn't a party; it's people. I found the people again in the days of the great picnics, and they listened to me; they believed in me once more and they made me their Prime Minister again."

Off in the distance, from away off in the town, they heard the long hoot of a train whistle. Sir John looked down at the children.

"Janet, David," he said quietly. "When I told Mr. Chadwick I would try to stop over in Perth for a few minutes today, he wanted me to make a speech at his picnic, even though he couldn't be there himself to hear it."

"Yes," sighed Mr. Chadwick, "it would have been something for them to remember. The last of the great picnics."

"Then the storm came up, and now there isn't time. But I've had an hour with an old friend. And with two bonnie children. That's more important than any speech. After all, I have made so many."

The lines of his face crinkled in a warm smile.

"But now that I have an audience," he said, "I find a bit of a speech coming on. Not a long one," he added hastily. "And just for you."

Sir John's hands gripped the wide lapels of his coat. He drew a deep breath, and stood proud and erect before them.

"Today," he said, "is the First of July. Your country's birthday. A birthday which belongs to us all."

He paused. His head went back. He spoke out strongly and clearly, as if to invisible listeners far away in space and time.

"And because it belongs to us all, as the years go by, I ask you to remember always what it means. The day of Confederation. The day your country was born." His voice rang. "Never let it be cheapened. Never let it be forgotten or ignored. And honor it always, for it is your country's day!"

There was a long silence. It was broken by another mournful, distant hoot from the engine of the waiting train.

Sir John drew a big gold watch from his waistcoat pocket. The cover snapped open.

"It's time to go," he said.

142

Independence Day

We hold these truths to be self-evident, that all men are created equal, that they are endowed by their Creator with certain unalienable Rights, that among these are Life, Liberty and the pursuit of Happiness.—

That to secure these rights, Governments are instituted among Men, deriving their just powers from the consent of the governed.

The Declaration of Independence

Independence Day is the birthday of the United States and our greatest national holiday. It commemorates the day, July 4, 1776, when the Declaration of Independence was adopted by the Continental Congress meeting in Philadelphia.

On July 8, 1776, the Liberty Bell, with its prophetic inscription "Proclaim Liberty throughout all the land," rang out from Independence Hall in Philadelphia to call the people to hear the Declaration read aloud. Bells pealed all day and far into the night, and postriders carried the news to other states and to General Washington, encamped with his troops in New York. The rule of King George of Great Britain over the American colonies was ended.

A parchment copy of the Declaration of Independence was signed on August 2, 1776, by fifty members of the Congress. This document is displayed in the National Archives Building in Washington, D.C.

Thomas Jefferson, who was to be the third President of the United States, wrote most of the Declaration, although John Adams, Benjamin Franklin, Robert Livingston, and Roger Sherman had also been appointed to prepare the draft.

143

On each anniversary of Independence Day it is well to re-affirm our faith in the rights Jefferson so brilliantly stated. We are glad that he included the "pursuit of Happiness" as well as the rights of liberty and life. It is a time, too, to think of the men and women who with faith, courage, and sacrifice engaged in a war against great odds and won a victory. Among the patriots whose stories can appropriately be read are George Washington, John Hancock, Thomas Paine, Richard Henry Lee, Patrick Henry, Samuel Adams, Paul Revere, as well as Thomas Jefferson, Benjamin Franklin, and John Adams. The young Frenchman, Lafayette, and the Polish patriot, Thaddeus Kosciusko, share in this valiant period.

The Fourth of July—the Glorious Fourth, as orators often proclaim it—is celebrated with flags waving, bells ringing, and displays of fireworks arching into the sky. There are speeches, parades, and picnics on hot July afternoons. Chicken to fry on the Fourth of July is as traditional as turkey for Thanksgiving.

When preparations were being made in 1826 to celebrate the fiftieth anniversary of Independence Day, ninety-one-year-old John Adams, our second President, was asked for a toast for the day. His response was "Independence now and Independence forever," a sentiment we can reaffirm on each new birthday of our nation.

Independence Day

Laura Ingalls Wilder

Almanzo was eating breakfast before he remembered that this was the Fourth of July. He felt more cheerful.

It was like Sunday morning. After breakfast he scrubbed his face with soft soap till it shone, and he parted his wet hair and combed it sleekly down. He put on his sheep's-gray trousers and his shirt of French calico, and his vest and his short round coat.

Mother had made his new suit in the new style. The coat fastened at the throat with a little flap of cloth, then the two sides slanted back to show his vest, and they rounded off over his trousers' pockets.

He put on his round straw hat, which Mother had made of braided oat-straws, and he was all dressed up for Independence Day. He felt very fine.

Father's shining horses were hitched to the shining, red-wheeled buggy, and they all drove away in the cool sunshine. All the country had a holiday air. Nobody was working in the fields, and along the road the people in their Sunday clothes were driving to town.

145

Father's swift horses passed them all. They passed by wagons and carts and buggies. They passed gray horses and black horses and dappled-gray horses. Almanzo waved his hat whenever he sailed past anyone he knew, and he would have been perfectly happy if only he had been driving that swift, beautiful team.

At the church sheds in Malone he helped Father unhitch. Mother and the girls and Royal hurried away. But Almanzo would rather help with the horses than do anything else. He couldn't drive them, but he could tie their halters and buckle on their blankets, and stroke their soft noses and give them hay.

Then he went out with Father and they walked on the crowded sidewalks. All the stores were closed, but ladies and gentlemen were walking up and down and talking. Ruffled little girls carried parasols, and all the boys were dressed up, like Almanzo. Flags were everywhere, and in the Square the band was playing "Yankee Doodle." The fifes tooted and the flutes shrilled and the drums came in with rub-a-dub-dub.

> "Yankee Doodle went to town,
> Riding on a pony,
> He stuck a feather in his hat,
> And called it macaroni!"

Even grown-ups had to keep time to it. And there, in the corner of the Square, were the two brass cannons!

The Square was not really square. The railroad made it three-cornered. But everybody called it the Square, anyway. It was fenced, and grass grew there. Benches stood in rows on the grass, and people were filing between the benches and sitting down as they did in church.

Almanzo went with Father to one of the best front seats. All the

146

important men stopped to shake hands with Father. The crowd kept coming till all the seats were full, and still there were people outside the fence.

The band stopped playing, and the minister prayed. Then the band tuned up again and everybody rose. Men and boys took off their hats. The band played, and everybody sang.

"Oh, say, can you see by the dawn's early light,

What so proudly we hailed at the twilight's last gleaming,

Whose broad stripes and bright stars through the perilous night,

O'er the ramparts we watched were so gallantly streaming?"

From the top of the flagpole, up against the blue sky, the Stars and Stripes were fluttering. Everybody looked at the American flag, and Almanzo sang with all his might.

Then everyone sat down, and a Congressman stood up on the platform. Slowly and solemnly he read the Declaration of Independence.

"When in the course of human events it becomes necessary for one people...to assume among the powers of the earth the separate and equal station....We hold these truths to be self-evident, that all men are created equal...."

Almanzo felt solemn and very proud.

Then two men made long political speeches. One believed in high tariffs, and one believed in free trade. All the grown-ups listened hard, but Almanzo did not understand the speeches very well and he began to be hungry. He was glad when the band played again.

The music was so gay; the bandsmen in their blue and red and their brass buttons tootled merrily, and the fat drummer beat rat-a-tat-tat on the drum. All the flags were fluttering and everybody was happy, because they were free and independent and this was Independence Day. And it was time to eat dinner.

Almanzo helped Father feed the horses while Mother and the girls spread the picnic lunch on the grass in the churchyard. Many others were picnicking there, too, and after he had eaten all he could Almanzo went back to the Square.

There was a lemonade stand by the hitching posts. A man sold pink lemonade, a nickel a glass, and a crowd of the town boys were standing around him. Cousin Frank was there. Almanzo had a drink at the town pump, but Frank said he was going to buy lemonade. He had a nickel. He walked up to the stand and bought a glass of the pink lemonade and drank it slowly. He smacked his lips and rubbed his stomach and said:

"Mmmm! Why don't you buy some?"

"Where'd you get the nickel?" Almanzo asked. He had never had a nickel. Father gave him a penny every Sunday to put in the collection-box in church; he had never had any other money.

"My father gave it to me," Frank bragged. "My father gives me a nickel every time I ask him."

"Well, so would my father if I asked him," said Almanzo.

"Well, why don't you ask him?" Frank did not believe that Father would give Almanzo a nickel. Almanzo did not know whether Father would, or not.

"Because I don't want to," he said.

"He wouldn't give you a nickel," Frank said.

"He would, too."

"I dare you to ask him," Frank said. The other boys were listening. Almanzo put his hands in his pockets and said:

"I'd just as lief ask him if I wanted to."

"Yah, you're scared!" Frank jeered. "Double dare! Double dare!"

148

Father was a little way down the street, talking to Mr. Paddock, the wagon-maker. Almanzo walked slowly toward them. He was fainthearted, but he had to go. The nearer he got to Father, the more he dreaded asking for a nickel. He had never before thought of doing such a thing. He was sure Father would not give it to him.

He waited till Father stopped talking and looked at him.

"What is it, son?" Father asked.

Almanzo was scared. "Father," he said.

"Well, son?"

"Father," Almanzo said, "would you—would you give me—a nickel?"

He stood there while Father and Mr. Paddock looked at him, and he wished he could get away. Finally Father asked:

"What for?"

Almanzo looked down at his moccasins and muttered:

"Frank had a nickel. He bought pink lemonade."

"Well," Father said, slowly, "if Frank treated you, it's only right you should treat him." Father put his hand in his pocket. Then he stopped and asked:

"Did Frank treat you to lemonade?"

Almanzo wanted so badly to get the nickel that he nodded. Then he squirmed and said:

"No, Father."

Father looked at him a long time. Then he took out his wallet and opened it, and slowly he took out a round, big silver half-dollar. He asked:

"Almanzo, do you know what this is?"

"Half a dollar," Almanzo answered.

"Yes. But do you know what half a dollar is?"

Almanzo didn't know it was anything but half a dollar.

"It's work, son," Father said. "That's what money is; it's hard work."

Mr. Paddock chuckled. "The boy's too young, Wilder," he said. "You can't make a youngster understand that."

"Almanzo's smarter than you think," said Father.

Almanzo didn't understand at all. He wished he could get away. But Mr. Paddock was looking at Father just as Frank looked at Almanzo when he double-dared him, and Father had said Almanzo was smart, so Almanzo tried to look like a smart boy. Father asked:

"You know how to raise potatoes, Almanzo?"

"Yes," Almanzo said.

"Say you have a seed potato in the spring, what do you do with it?"

"You cut it up," Almanzo said.

"Go on, son."

"Then you harrow—first you manure the field, and plow it. Then you harrow, and mark the ground. And plant the potatoes, and plow them, and hoe them. You plow and hoe them twice."

"That's right, son. And then?"

"Then you dig them and put them down cellar."

"Yes. Then you pick them over all winter; you throw out all the little ones and the rotten ones. Come spring, you load them up and haul them here to Malone, and you sell them. And if you get a good price, son, how much do you get to show for all that work? How much do you get for half a bushel of potatoes?"

"Half a dollar," Almanzo said.

"Yes," said Father. "That's what's in this half-dollar, Almanzo. The work that raised half a bushel of potatoes is in it."

150

Almanzo looked at the round piece of money that Father held up. It looked small, compared with all that work.

"You can have it, Almanzo," Father said. Almanzo could hardly believe his ears. Father gave him the heavy half-dollar.

"It's yours," said Father. "You could buy a sucking pig with it, if you want to. You could raise it, and it would raise a litter of pigs, worth four, five dollars apiece. Or you can trade that half-dollar for lemonade, and drink it up. You do as you want, it's your money."

Almanzo forgot to say thank you. He held the half-dollar a minute, then he put his hand in his pocket and went back to the boys by the lemonade stand. The man was calling out,

"Step this way, step this way! Ice-cold lemonade, pink lemonade, only five cents a glass! Only half a dime, ice-cold pink lemonade! The twentieth part of a dollar!"

Frank asked Almanzo:

"Where's the nickel?"

"He didn't give me a nickel," said Almanzo, and Frank yelled:

"Yah, yah! I told you he wouldn't! I told you so!"

"He gave me half a dollar," said Almanzo.

The boys wouldn't believe it till he showed them. Then they crowded around, waiting for him to spend it. He showed it to them all, and put it back in his pocket.

"I'm going to look around," he said, "and buy me a good little sucking pig."

The band came marching down the street, and they all ran along beside it. The flag was gloriously waving in front, then came the buglers blowing and the fifers tootling and the drummer rattling the drumsticks on the drum. Up the street and down the street went the band, with all the boys following it, and then it stopped in the

Square by the brass cannons.

Hundreds of people were there, crowding to watch.

The cannons sat on their haunches, pointing their long barrels upward. The band kept on playing. Two men kept shouting, "Stand back! Stand back!" and other men were pouring black powder into the cannons' muzzles and pushing it down with wads of cloth on long rods.

The iron rods had two handles, and two men pushed and pulled on them, driving the black powder down the brass barrels. Then all the boys ran to pull grass and weeds along the railroad tracks. They carried them by armfuls to the cannons, and the men crowded the weeds into the cannons' muzzles and drove them down with the long rods.

A bonfire was burning by the railroad tracks, and long iron rods were heating in it.

When all the weeds and grass had been packed tight against the powder in the cannons, a man took a little more powder in his hand and carefully filled the two little touchholes in the barrels. Now everybody was shouting,

"Stand back! Stand back!"

Mother took hold of Almanzo's arm and made him come away with her. He told her:

"Aw, Mother, they're only loaded with powder and weeds. I won't get hurt, Mother. I'll be careful, honest." But she made him come away from the cannons.

Two men took the long iron rods from the fire. Everybody was still, watching. Standing as far behind the cannons as they could, the two men stretched out the rods and touched their red-hot tips to the touchholes. A little flame like a candle flame flickered up from the powder. The little flames stood there burning; nobody breathed. Then—BOOM!

The cannons leaped backward, the air was full of flying grass and weeds. Almanzo ran with all the other boys to feel the warm muzzles of the cannons. Everybody was exclaiming about what a loud noise they had made.

"That's the noise that made the Redcoats run!" Mr. Paddock said to Father.

"Maybe," Father said, tugging his beard. "But it was muskets that won the Revolution. And don't forget it was axes and plows that made this country."

"That's so, come to think of it," Mr. Paddock said.

Independence Day was over. The cannons had been fired, and there was nothing more to do but hitch up the horses and drive home to do the chores.

That night when they were going to the house with the milk, Almanzo asked Father,

"Father, how was it axes and plows that made this country? Didn't we fight England for it?"

"We fought for Independence, son," Father said. "But all the land our forefathers had was a little strip of country, here between the mountains and the ocean. All the way from here west was Indian country, and Spanish and French and English country. It was farmers that took all that country and made it America."

"How?" Almanzo asked.

"Well, son, the Spaniards were soldiers, and high-and-mighty gentlemen that only wanted gold. And the French were fur traders, wanting to make quick money. And England was busy fighting wars. But we were farmers, son; we wanted the land. It was farmers that went over the mountains, and cleared the land, and settled it, and farmed it, and hung on to their farms.

"This country goes three thousand miles west, now. It goes 'way out beyond Kansas, and beyond the Great American Desert, over mountains bigger than these mountains, and down to the Pacific Ocean. It's the biggest country in the world, and it was farmers who took all that country and made it America, son. Don't you ever forget that."

Fireworks

James Reeves

They rise like sudden fiery flowers
    That burst upon the night,
Then fall to earth in burning showers
    Of crimson, blue, and white.

Like buds too wonderful to name,
    Each miracle unfolds,
And catherine wheels begin to flame
    Like whirling marigolds.

Rockets and Roman candles make
    An orchard of the sky,
Whence magic trees their petals shake
    Upon each gazing eye.

154

AUGUST

Birthdays

OBSERVED THROUGHOUT THE YEAR

If you can blow out all the candles on your birthday cake with one puff, the wish you make will come true.

—An old birthday custom

All children have one special day in the year, their birthdays, a day for family and friends and love.

Mother and Father never forget their birthday child. Their girl or boy's special day is a time for congratulations and good wishes, for fun, games, gifts homemade or purchased, perhaps a party with ice cream and favors, and most of all, a cake.

When the magical moment comes, the cake is brought in, usually frosted and aflutter with tiny points of light, to be set before the birthday girl or boy. Then everyone sings "Happy birthday to you!" and with a puff the candles are snuffed out. A new year's begun!

Of course birthdays come in every month of the year, but because August has no official holidays, let's call it among ourselves the time to remember birthdays.

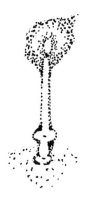

Who Wants a Birthday?

David McCord

Who wants a birthday?
Somebody does.

"I *am*," says a birthday,
But never "I *was.*"

"Five, six," says a birthday:
"You're seven!" "You're nine!"

"I'm yours," says a birthday,
"And you, child, are mine."

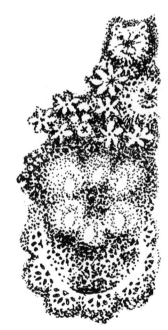

"*How* old?" says a birthday.
(You have to guess right.)

"You're *what?*" says a birthday.
(You may be: you *might.*)

"A cake," says a birthday,
"I'm sure there's a cake!"

"A wish," says a birthday,
"What wish do you make?"

"I'm glad," says a birthday,
"To see how you've grown."

"Hello!" says a birthday.
("Hello!" says my own.)

Pippi Celebrates Her Birthday

Astrid Lindgren,
translated by Florence Lamborn

In creating Pippi Longstocking, Astrid Lindgren, the
Swedish writer, introduced an amusing heroine, an orphan whose
father was a sailor. Pippi lives with her horse and her pet monkey,
Mr. Nilsson, who came from her father's ship.

One day Tommy and Annika found a letter in their mailbox.

It was addressed to TMMY and ANIKA, and when they opened it they found a card which read:

> TMMY AND ANIKA ARE INVITED TO PIPPI'S
> TOMORO TO HER BERTHDAY PARTY. DRES:
> WARE WATEVER YOU LIK.

Tommy and Annika were so happy they began to skip and dance. They understood perfectly well what was printed on the card although the spelling was a little unusual. Pippi had had a great deal of trouble writing it. To be sure, she had not recognized the letter "i" in school the day she was there, but all the same she could write a little. When she was sailing on the ocean one of the sailors on her father's ship used to take her up on deck in the evening now and then and try to teach her to write. Unfortunately Pippi was not a very patient pupil. All of a sudden she would say, "No, Fridolf"—that was his name—"no, Fridolf, bother all this learning! I can't study any more now because I must climb the mast to see what kind of weather we're going to have tomorrow."

So it was no wonder the writing didn't go so well now. One whole night she sat struggling with that invitation, and at dawn, just as the stars were paling in the sky over Villa Villekulla, she tiptoed over to Tommy's and Annika's house and dropped the letter into their mailbox.

As soon as Tommy and Annika came home from school they began to get all dressed up for the party. Annika asked her mother to curl her hair, and her mother did, and tied it with a big pink satin bow. Tommy combed his hair with water so that it would lie all nice and smooth. He certainly didn't want any curls. Then Annika wanted to put on her very best dress, but her mother thought she'd better not for she was seldom neat and clean when she came home from Pippi's; so Annika had to be satisfied with her next best dress. Tommy didn't care what suit he wore so long as he looked nice.

Of course they had bought a present for Pippi. They had taken the money out of their own piggy banks, and on the way home from school had run into the toy shop on Main Street and bought a very beautiful — well, what they had bought was a secret for the time being. There it lay, wrapped in green paper and tied with a great deal of string, and when they were ready Tommy took the package, and off they went, followed by their mother's warning to take good care of their clothes. Annika was to carry the package part of the way, and they were both to hold it when they handed it to Pippi—that they had agreed upon.

It was already November, and dusk came early. When Tommy and Annika went in through the gate of Villa Villekulla they held each other's hands tightly, because it was quite dark in Pippi's garden and the wind sighed mournfully through the bare old trees. "Seems like fall," said Tommy. It was so much pleasanter to see the lighted windows in Villa Villekulla and to know that they were going to a birthday party.

Ordinarily Tommy and Annika rushed in through the kitchen door, but this time they went to the front door. The horse was not on the porch. Tommy gave a lively knock on the door.

From inside came a low voice:

> *"Who comes in the dark night*
> *On the road to my house?*
> *Is it a ghost or just*
> *A poor little mouse?"*

"No, no, Pippi, it's us," shrieked Annika. "Open the door!"
Pippi opened the door.

"Oh, Pippi, why did you say that about a ghost? I was so scared," said Annika and completely forgot to congratulate Pippi.

Pippi laughed heartily and opened the door to the kitchen. How good it was to come in where it was light and warm! The birthday party was to be in the kitchen, because that was the pleasantest room in the house. There were only two other rooms on the first floor, the parlor in which there was only one piece of furniture and Pippi's bedroom. The kitchen was large and roomy, and Pippi had scrubbed it until it shone. She had put rugs on the floor and a large new cloth on the table. She had embroidered the cloth herself with flowers that certainly looked most remarkable, but Pippi declared that such flowers grew in Farthest India, so of course that made them all right. The curtains were drawn and the fire burned merrily. On the woodbox sat Mr. Nilsson, banging pot lids together. In a corner stood the horse, for he too had been invited to the party.

Now at last Tommy and Annika remembered that they were supposed to congratulate Pippi. Tommy bowed and Annika curtsied and then they handed Pippi the green package and said, "May we congratulate you and wish you a happy birthday?" Pippi thanked them and eagerly tore the package open. And there was a music box! Pippi was wild with delight. She patted Tommy and she patted Annika and she patted the music box and she patted the wrapping paper. She wound up the music box, and with much plinking and plonking out came a melody that was probably supposed to be "Ack, du käre Augustin."

Pippi wound and wound and seemed to forget everything else. But suddenly she remembered something. "Oh, my goodness, you must have your birthday presents too!" she said.

"But it isn't our birthday," said Tommy and Annika.

Pippi stared at them in amazement. "No, but it's my birthday, isn't it? And so I can give birthday presents too, can't I? Or does it say in your schoolbooks that such a thing can't be done? Is it something to do with that old pluttifikation that makes it impossible?"

"Oh, of course it's possible," said Tommy. "It just isn't customary. But for my part, I'd be very glad to have a present."

"Me too," said Annika.

Pippi ran into the parlor and brought back two packages from the chest. When Tommy opened his he found a little ivory flute, and in Annika's package was a lovely brooch shaped like a butterfly. The wings of the butterfly were set with blue and red and green stones.

When they had all had their birthday presents it was time to sit down at the table, where there were all sorts of cakes and buns. The cakes were rather peculiar in shape, but Pippi declared they were just the kind of cakes they had in China.

Pippi served hot chocolate with whipped cream, and the children were just about to begin their feast when Tommy said, "When Mamma and Papa have a party the gentlemen always get cards telling them what ladies to take in to dinner. I should think we ought to have cards too."

"Okay," said Pippi.

"Although it will be kind of hard for us because I'm the only gentleman here," added Tommy doubtfully.

"Fiddlesticks," said Pippi. "Do you think Mr. Nilsson is a lady, maybe?"

"Oh, of course not, I forgot Mr. Nilsson," said Tommy, and he sat down on the woodbox and wrote on a card:

"*Mr. Settergren will have the pleasure of taking Miss Longstocking in to dinner.*"

"Mr. Settergren, that's me," said he with satisfaction and showed Pippi the card. Then he wrote on the next card:

"*Mr. Nilsson will have the pleasure of taking Miss Settergren in to dinner.*"

"Okay, but the horse must have a card too," said Pippi decidedly, "even if he can't sit at the table."

So Tommy, at Pippi's dictation, wrote:

"The horse will have the pleasure of remaining in the corner where he will be served cakes and sugar."

Pippi held the card under the horse's nose and said, "Read this and see what you think of it."

As the horse had no objection to make, Tommy offered Pippi his arm, and they walked to the table. Mr. Nilsson showed no intention of offering his arm to Annika, so she took a firm hold of him and lifted him up to the table. But he didn't want to sit on a chair; he insisted on sitting right on the table. Nor did he want any chocolate with whipped cream, but when Pippi poured water in his cup he took it in both his hands and drank.

Annika and Tommy and Pippi ate and ate, and Annika said that if these cakes were the kind they had in China then she intended to move to China when she grew up.

When Mr. Nilsson had emptied his cup he turned it upside down and put it on his head. When Pippi saw that, she did the same, but as she had not drunk quite all her chocolate a little stream ran down her forehead and over her nose. She caught it with her tongue and lapped it all up.

"Waste not, want not," she said.

Tommy and Annika licked their cups clean before they put them on their heads.

When everybody had had enough and the horse had had his share, Pippi took hold of all four corners of the tablecloth and lifted it up so that the cups and plates tumbled over each other as if they were in a sack. Then she stuffed the whole bundle in the woodbox.

"I always like to tidy up a little as soon as I have eaten," she said.

Then it was time for games. Pippi suggested that they play a game called "Don't touch the floor." It was very simple. The only thing one had to do was walk all around the kitchen without once stepping on the floor. Pippi skipped around in the twinkling of an eye, and even for Tommy and Annika it was quite easy. You began on the drainboard, and if you stretched your legs enough it was possible to step onto the back of the stove. From the stove to the woodbox, and from the woodbox to the hat shelf, and down onto the table, and from there across two chairs to the corner cupboard. Between the corner cupboard and the drainboard was a distance of several feet, but, luckily, there stood the horse, and if you climbed up on him at the tail end and slid off at the head end, making a quick turn at exactly the right moment, you landed exactly on the drainboard.

When they had played this game for a while and Annika's dress was no longer her next-best dress but her next-next-next-best one, and Tommy had become as black as a chimney sweep, then they decided to think up something else.

"Suppose we go up in the attic and visit the ghosts," suggested Pippi.

Annika gasped. "A-a-are there really ghosts in the attic?" she asked.

"Are there ghosts? Millions!" said Pippi. "It's just swarming with all sorts of ghosts and spirits. You trip over them wherever you walk. Shall we go up?"

"Oh, Pippi!" said Annika and looked reproachfully at her.

"Mamma says there aren't any such things as ghosts and

164

goblins," said Tommy boldly.

"And well she might," said Pippi, "because there aren't any anywhere else. All the ghosts in the world live in my attic. And it doesn't pay to try to make them move. But they aren't dangerous. They just pinch you in the arm so you get black and blue, and they howl, and they play ninepins with their heads."

"Do—do—do they really play n-n-ninepins with their heads?"

"Sure, that's just what they do," said Pippi. "Come on, let's go up and talk with them. I'm good at playing n-n-ninepins."

Tommy didn't want to show that he was frightened, and in a way he really did want to see a ghost. That would be something to tell the boys at school! Besides, he consoled himself with the thought that the ghosts probably wouldn't dare to hurt Pippi. He decided to go along. Poor Annika didn't want to go under any circumstances, but then she happened to think that a little tiny ghost might sneak downstairs while she was sitting alone in the kitchen. That decided the matter. Better to be with Pippi and Tommy among thousands of ghosts than alone in the kitchen with even the tiniest little ghost child.

Pippi went first. She opened the door to the attic stairs. It was pitch-dark there. Tommy took a firm grip on Pippi, and Annika took an even firmer grip on Tommy, and so they went up. The stairs creaked and squeaked with every step. Tommy began to wonder if it wouldn't have been better to stay down in the kitchen, and Annika didn't need to wonder—she was sure of it. At last they came to the top of the stairs and stood in the attic. It was pitch-dark there too, except where a little moonbeam shone on the floor. There were sighs and mysterious noises in every corner when the wind blew in through the cracks.

"Hi, all you ghosts!" shrieked Pippi.

But if there was any ghost there he certainly didn't answer.

"Well, I might have known," said Pippi, "they've gone to a council meeting of the Ghost and Goblin Society."

Annika sighed with relief and hoped that the meeting would last a long time. But just then an awful sound came from one of the corners of the attic.

"Whoo-ooo-ooo!" it said, and a moment later Tommy saw something come rushing toward him in the dimness. He felt it brush his forehead and saw something disappear through a little window that stood open.

He shrieked to high heaven, "A ghost! A ghost!"

And Annika shrieked with him.

"That poor thing will be late for the meeting," said Pippi. "If it was ghost. And not an owl. For that matter, there aren't any ghosts," she continued after a while. "If anybody insists that there are ghosts, I'll tweak him in the nose."

"Yes, but you said so yourself," said Annika.

"Is that so? Did I?" said Pippi. "Well, then I'll certainly tweak my own nose."

And she took a firm grip on her nose and tweaked it.

After that Tommy and Annika felt a little calmer. In fact they were now so courageous that they ventured to go up to the window and look out over the garden. Big dark clouds sailed through the sky and did their best to hide the moon. And the wind sighed in the trees.

Tommy and Annika turned around. But then—oh, horrors—they saw a white figure coming toward them.

"A ghost!" shrieked Tommy wildly.

Annika was so scared she couldn't even shriek. The ghost came nearer and nearer. Tommy and Annika hugged each other and shut their eyes.

But then they heard the ghost say, "Look what I found! Papa's nightshirt in an old sea chest over here. If I hem it up around the bottom I can wear it."

Pippi came up to them with the nightshirt dangling around her legs.

"Oh, Pippi, I could have died of fright," said Annika.

"But nightshirts aren't dangerous," Pippi assured her. "They don't bite anybody except in self-defense."

Pippi now decided to examine the sea chest thoroughly. She lifted it up and carried it over to the window and opened the cover, so that what little moonlight there was fell on the contents of the chest. There were a great many old clothes, which she threw out on the attic floor. There were a telescope, a few books, three pistols, a sword, and a bag of goldpieces.

"Tiddelipom and piddeliday," said Pippi contentedly.

"It's so exciting!" said Tommy.

Pippi gathered everything in the nightshirt, and down they went into the kitchen again. Annika was perfectly satisfied to leave the attic.

"Never let children handle firearms," said Pippi and took a pistol in each hand and prepared to fire. "Otherwise some accident can easily happen," she said, shooting off both pistols at once. "That was a good bang," she announced and looked up in the ceiling. The bullets had made two holes.

"Who knows?" she said hopefully. "Perhaps the bullets have gone right through the ceiling and hit some ghosts in the legs. That will teach them to think twice before they set out to scare any innocent little children again. Because even if there aren't any ghosts, they don't need to go round scaring folks out of their wits, I should think. Would you each like a pistol?" she asked.

Tommy was enchanted, and Annika also very much wanted a pistol, provided it wasn't loaded.

"Now we can organize a robber band if we want to," said Pippi. She held the telescope up to her eyes. "With this I can almost see the fleas in South America, I think," she continued. "And it'll be good to have if we do organize a robber band."

Just then there was a knock at the door. It was Tommy's and Annika's father, who had come to take them home. It was long past their bedtime, he said. Tommy and Annika hurried to say thank you, bid Pippi good-by, and collect all their belongings, the flute, the brooch, and the pistols.

Pippi followed her guests out to the porch and watched them disappear through the garden. They turned around to wave. The light from inside shone on her. There she stood with her stiff red braids, dressed in her father's nightshirt which billowed around her feet. In one hand she held a pistol and in the other the sword. She saluted with it.

When Tommy and Annika and their father reached the gate they heard her calling. They stopped to listen. The wind whistled through the trees so they could just barely hear what she said.

"I'm going to be a pirate when I grow up," she cried. "Are you?"

SEPTEMBER

Labor Day

OBSERVED ON THE FIRST MONDAY IN SEPTEMBER

Labor Day, a popular holiday in Canada and Puerto Rico as well as in the United States, comes at summer's end, the blooming of the goldenrod, the return to school classes and fall activities.

Labor Day honors all who work, whether in industry, on the farm, in business, education, arts, or the professions. It is celebrated with parades, cookouts, sports, rest, and recreation. But the holiday has deeper meaning. It stands for the labor movement in the United States, an important force in American life. It stands for the labor leaders who strove to obtain better working conditions, higher pay, and better lives for workers, their families and our nation as a whole.

Labor Day goes back to 1882, when Peter J. McGuire, president of the United Brotherhood of Carpenters, proposed a national holiday to honor workers and win recognition for the contribution labor makes to the dignity and prosperity of life in America. That same year, the first Labor Day parade was held in New York City, but it was not until 1894 that the day became a national holiday.

Stories about the lives and achievements of labor leaders are appropriate to share during the Labor Day period. Among names that might be included are Samuel Gompers, John L. Lewis, A. Philip Randolph, Cesar Chavez, and Frances Perkins, who as United States Secretary of Labor was the first woman to become a Cabinet member. It is also suitable to read biographies of scientists and inventors such as Thomas A. Edison and George Washington Carver.

I Hear America Singing

Walt Whitman

I hear America singing, the varied carols I hear,
Those of mechanics, each one singing his as it should be blithe
and strong,
The carpenter singing his as he measures his plank or beam,
The mason singing his as he makes ready for work or leaves
off work,
The boatman singing what belongs to him in his boat, the
deckhand singing on the steamboat deck,
The shoemaker singing as he sits on his bench, the hatter singing
as he stands.
The wood-cutter's song, the ploughboy's on his way in the
morning, or at noon intermission or at sundown,
The delicious singing of the mother, or of the young wife at work,
or of the girl sewing or washing,
Each singing what belongs to him or her and to none else,
The day what belongs to the day—at night the party of young
fellows, robust, friendly,
Singing with open mouths their strong melodious songs.

Down-to-Earth Dreamer

Margaret Cousins

At the age of twelve, Thomas Alva Edison was a train-boy, selling newspapers, oranges, and candy on the Grand Trunk Railway between Port Huron and Detroit, Michigan. He grew up to be the "hero of invention" and lived to see the world celebrate the fiftieth anniversary of his invention of the electric light. The phonograph and motion pictures are also his inventions. As one of the American heroes of success, his life is an appropriate Labor Day story.

Thomas Edison was often called the greatest genius of his age. There are few men of any age who have had a more direct effect on the lives of everyone everywhere than the inventor of the first practical electric light. But Edison never considered it a compliment to be described as a genius.

"There is no such thing as genius," Edison said. "What people choose to call genius is simply hard work—one per cent inspiration and ninety-nine per cent perspiration."

172

But Edison was also a dreamer. From his earliest childhood he was fascinated by the secrets of nature. "Nature is full of mysteries," he often said. He brooded on these mysteries and tried to understand the secrets and figure out what he could do with them. He enjoyed thinking. "There are few things people won't do to avoid the labor of thinking," Edison said. "Unfortunately, thinking is the hardest work in the world for those who have not formed the habit. But thinking can give excitement and pleasure."

Edison could not imagine being bored. As he loved to think, he also loved to work. On his seventy-fifth birthday, he was asked what his philosophy of life was. "Work," he said, "bringing out the secrets of nature and applying them for the happiness of man." On that occasion he said that he had enough inventions in mind to keep him busy for another hundred years.

Edison suffered many privations in his early life and he knew disappointment and defeat, but he never thought of feeling sorry for himself. "You might as well look on the bright side," he said. He ascribed some of his remarkable power of concentration to his deafness. "Think of all the nonsense I haven't had to listen to by not being able to hear it," he said.

Edison took pride in his accomplishments when his inventions succeeded and benefited others. He understood the importance of publicity to bring his useful work to the attention of the public. But he was always modest. He appreciated the honors given him but would have worked on without them, or without recognition of any kind....

Edison did not believe in worry. He was too busy to worry about what might happen. He was more interested in making something happen. When things did not work out to suit him, he did not worry about what had happened. "I have no interest in spilt milk," he said.

As a leader, Edison inspired loyalty in the men who worked for him. He asked more than they could give, and they all wanted to please him. He never asked them to do what he couldn't or wouldn't do. He had endless patience. But his disposition was changeable. He loved jokes. He whistled, sang and laughed at work. But he also had a quick temper. He could not forgive people who slighted their work or did not insist, as he did, on the highest quality of performance....

Between 1869 and 1910, the inventor's years of greatest achievement, Edison applied for 1,328 separate and distinct patents. He made many inventions which he did not attempt to patent — inventions which he left unpatented and simply gave to the public. There was little in the world that did not interest him. He could carry on many different types of research at the same time. He could work on unimportant things with the same zest and enthusiasm he gave to important things. For several weeks at one time, he was interested in creating a doll that could talk. Edison spent considerable time playing with his phonographic dolls.

Edison was a man of ideas. But he did not believe that there was anything unusual about his ability to have ideas. He said that anybody could have ideas who was willing to observe, study and think. He believed that people should start as early as possible to look at the world and nature and to draw conclusions about what they saw. "Thinking is a habit," he said over and over. "If you do not learn to think when you are young, you may never learn." He never denied that he made guesses. Guesswork or hunches, proved out by experiment, may become invention, he said.

"Imagination supplies the ideas," Edison said. "Technical knowledge carries them out. Unless ideas are carried out they are useless."...

Edison believed in education. Self-educated, he knew the value of learning. "Education isn't play—and it can't be made to look like play," he said. "It is hard, hard work. But it can be made interesting work."...

Edison believed in America. When he was decorated by other governments, he always said that he felt the honor was not for him but for his country....When Edison was awarded the Congressional Medal of Honor in 1928, he was called the most useful American citizen.

In June, 1961, Thomas Edison took his place among the American immortals in the Hall of Fame at New York University. Perhaps no one has more truly deserved this honor. He typified the American ideal in his determination to harness the secrets of nature for the benefit of all people everywhere. He recognized that the measure of life is not what we get but what we give.

Whenever the tiniest filament of electric light glimmers in darkness, Thomas Alva Edison's work lives after him.

American Indian Day

A number of states have special holidays designated American Indian Day. New York was the first to proclaim such a day, in 1916, giving public recognition to the contribution of the American Indian. There had been earlier efforts to support such a day. Red Fox James, of the Blackfoot Indians, had sought in 1914 the aid of state governors to sponsor a national Indian Day. In 1915, Sherman Coolidge, of the Arapaho tribe, president of the American Indian Association, made a formal request for such a day.

Girls and boys find that interest in the history and lore of the American Indian leads down fascinating trails. When we show appreciation of the American Indian we recognize that these native Americans had distinctive civilizations and cultures long before Europeans arrived.

The Indian way of living was in harmony with nature. To the Indian, roots are important and strong family life is important. Tribal beliefs and customs pass from one generation to the next. Life and work are attuned to earth and sky, and they move to the rhythm of the seasons.

When we honor the American Indian we think of Samoset and Massasoit who received the Pilgrims with kindness, of Squanto and others who helped the Colonists during the first hard years in Plymouth. We remember leaders in war and peace: Tecumseh, orator and statesman in the post-Revolutionary period; Sacagawea, the Bird Woman, who guided Lewis and Clark on their expedition through the Dakotas and on to the Pacific Ocean; Chief Joseph of the Nez Percé, brave in defeat; Crazy Horse, Oglala Sioux whose figure is sculptured in granite in the Black Hills of South Dakota; Sequoya, the gifted Cherokee who invented a system of writing.

When we honor the Indian we recall American place names of Indian origin, Adirondack, Chicago, Mississippi. We see Indian emblems in the state flags of Oklahoma and New Mexico and find Indians pictured on several state seals. Indian words and phrases are part of our speech, words such as powwow, raccoon, and pumpkin; phrases such as to walk Indian file and Indian summer.

As we become aware of Indian life we see how cultures vary from place to place. We are sensitive to present-day struggles that center around building a better life for Indians and strengthening pride in a unique heritage.

When we honor the Indian, we think of contributions to art and handicraft, painting, basketry, pottery, weaving, and jewelry. We listen to music and learn to appreciate the ceremonial dances of the Southwest. As we read Indian prose and poetry with their beauty and wisdom we realize that the American Indian has woven a thread of vivid color into the tapestry of our national literature.

The War God's Horse Song

Navajo Indian

I am the Turquoise Woman's son.
On top of Belted Mountain
Beautiful horses—slim like a weasel!
My horse has a hoof like striped agate;
His fetlock is like a fine eagle-plume;
His legs are like quick lightning.
My horse's body is like an eagle-plumed arrow;
My horse has a tail like a trailing black cloud.
I put flexible goods on my horse's back;
The Little Holy Wind blows through his hair.

His mane is made of short rainbows.
My horse's ears are made of round corn.
My horse's eyes are made of big stars.
My horse's head is made of mixed waters
(From the holy springs—he never knows thirst).
My horse's teeth are made of white shell.
The long rainbow is in his mouth for a bridle,
        And with it I guide him.
When my horse neighs, different-colored horses follow.
When my horse neighs, different-colored sheep follow.
        I am wealthy, because of him.

Before me peaceful,
Behind me peaceful,
Under me peaceful,
Over me peaceful,
All around me peaceful—
Peaceful voice when he neighs.
I am Everlasting and Peaceful.
I stand for my horse.

Thunderbird

Henry Chafetz

When the earth was new, giants lived among the Indians. And the greatest of the giants that then walked the earth was Nasan. One hundred feet high Nasan stood, and each step he took was a mile long. Five feet wide was the space between his eyes, and his mouth when it was open seemed as large as a valley. His teeth looked like stumps of bright white birch trees when he smiled.

Nasan's dwelling place was at one end of the earth on a very high mountain facing the Eastern Ocean, and his lodge was on the

179

tallest peak of this mountain where the blue clouds met and passed each other. Nasan lived here all alone. He was a lonely giant.

One night, around the council fire of the giants, it was agreed that the Evening Star Lady was the fairest of all the women known to the great ones of the world. The Evening Star was lovely and bright to see, rising and shining in the sky each night.

The Indians respected and feared all the great beings — the Great Spirit, all the animal gods, all the bird gods, and the giants also — but they loved the Evening Star Lady.

She was many things to the Indians. Each night the calendar men of the tribes looked to the rising of the Evening Star as the time to make another cut in their calendar sticks. The wanderer, the war scout, and the hunter returning home late at night always looked forward to the Evening Star to guide them on the trail. And to her only, the young Indian lovers sang happy songs and told the secrets in their hearts.

Now, Nasan was lonely.

"A pity it is," he said to himself, "that I have no wife to mend my moccasins, to keep my lodge in order, and to cook for me."

The giant looked up in the sky at the Evening Star Lady. His heart leaped with delight as he beheld her brightness, and at once he knew he had a great love for her. Nasan was determined to have the Evening Star Lady for his wife.

The giant called for the old Needlewoman.

Out of the cave where she made her home came the one-eyed Needlewoman. She came with her witching needles, her magic loom, and her buckskin bag of medicine.

"Make me wings, Grandmother," Nasan said to the Needle-woman. "I wish to go on a journey to the sky."

180

The Needlewoman was very old. Her hair was white and her one good eye was gray and deep. Old she was, but her hands were quick-moving and her fingers nimble.

In mid-forest by the light of the moon, while animal and Indian slept, the Needlewoman made the wings.

She took one thousand feathers from one hundred wild birds, and she obtained the finest and strongest thread from the gray spiders who lived in the shadowy places of the Gloomy Hills where the mists linger. The Needlewoman stitched and hitched, and with the thread she bound the feathers together.

She deftly wove the silver of the moonbeams, the breath of a fleet deer, and the speed of a darting arrow into the wings.

The Needlewoman made a paint from the bark of a hemlock tree, and she colored the wings red.

She then dipped the wings in the waters of the Great Lake of Salt, and thus she made the wings strong.

Then the Needlewoman called for Nasan. Only a giant could carry these large and strong wings on his back. But Nasan was the greatest of the giants, and the wings fit him well.

Nasan soared like a big bird right up to the Evening Star Lady.

He brought her a buckskin bead bag and many white shells, and he dropped ermine skins and buffalo robes at her feet. Nasan promised the Evening Star Lady he would do anything she ever wished, if she would make her home in his lodge.

The Evening Star Lady smiled at the giant and put her arms around him. Off he flew with her to his mountain home.

The next night the Evening Star Lady did not appear in the sky. The night was gloomy.

The Indians looked and looked, but the Evening Star no longer shone in the sky at night. The night wanderers became lost, the calendar men could not keep the right time, and worst of all, the Indian lovers were dejected. Gone were their dreams, gone were their sweet songs, for gone was the Evening Star Lady, their star of love.

There was much sorrow among all the Indians. They assembled from near and far and cried out to the Great Spirit, who was the ruler of the sky:

"O Great Mystery, find and bring back for us the Evening Star Lady."

The Great Spirit looked over the edge of the sky and heard the cries of the Indians. The Great Spirit looked into his know-it-all medicine bag and saw that the Evening Star Lady had flown off with Nasan the giant.

The Great Spirit ordered Nasan to let the Evening Star Lady return to her place in the sky. But Nasan refused to give her up.

Now the Great Spirit was angry.

This was not good.

He swore an almighty oath to punish the giant.

The Great Spirit rattled his great war drum:

BOOM! BOOM! BOOM!

The Great Spirit sounded his war cry:

HI YI! HI YI! HI YI! YI! YI!

Now Nasan, being a giant, was also a wizard who knew mighty magic.

When he heard the Great Spirit's war cry, Nasan pulled up a tall pine tree out of the ground. He used the tree, as he would a pencil, to draw a circle around his lodge. Four times he drew a ring around his home, and by placing a strong charm over the inside of the circle, made it a magic zone where no harm could come to him.

The Great Spirit rode the winds to the mountain home of Nasan. With his hands he shook the mountain.

The grass flew and many trees fell as the mountain rocked. But the grass within the magic ring all around Nasan's lodge stood still, the trees were unshaken, and the giant's lodge did not fall.

The Great Spirit breathed upon the mountain.

His breath was fierce and burning, and out of it there came a roaring of fire and smoke that swept over the mountain, scorching all the land before it. But the fire crumbled to cold ashes at the edge of Nasan's charmed circle.

Truly, there was strong medicine in the giant's magic.

The Great Spirit sent five hundred dark shapes and weird forms to the home of Nasan. They could go no further than the outside of the circle. The Great Spirit sent cold and he sent floods. But these also failed to cross the edge of the ring. It was like a strong wall; nothing could pass it.

Now the Great Spirit, who knew everything, knew that the Evening Star Lady desired above all things a robe of white deerskin. Through the Evening Star Lady, then, he would lure Nasan out from the protection of the magic circle.

The Great Spirit went to the Chief of the Ants and instructed him what to do and say.

The Chief of the Ants took his people to the mountain where Nasan lived, and the ants began to eat holes in the mountain. They dug and dug their way upwards until they came right underneath the floor of Nasan's lodge.

That night, as Nasan and the Evening Star Lady lay down to sleep, they heard voices beneath them. The giant and the Evening Star Lady, like all the great beings, knew the languages of all creatures—whether human, bird, animal, or insect. Nasan and the Evening Star Lady put their ears to the earth floor of the lodge and the words of the ants reached them from the ground underneath their sleeping blankets.

"One must see this wondrous white deer for himself," said an ant.

"Is it really all white?" another ant asked.

"Whiter than snow, silver, or clouds. White beyond all belief is this deer."

The ants talked in very loud voices to make certain that Nasan and the Evening Star Lady would hear.

"Where does this more than snow-white deer live?" asked one ant.

"This astounding white deer runs wild and free in the nearby forest of the hemlock trees."

"Surely," another ant said, "it is the only white deer in the world."

The Evening Star Lady could not sleep that night knowing there was a white deer near by, and during the day she could not rest for thinking about the beautiful white robe its skin would make for her. The Evening Star Lady felt she could not live without such a robe.

"Husband," she said to Nasan, "I am most anxious for a white deerskin robe."

So great was Nasan's love for the Evening Star Lady, and so strong was her wish, that he agreed to go on a hunt for the white deer.

184

The giant set out down the mountain for the forest of the hemlock trees. He moved cautiously, knowing the Great Spirit was still on the warpath against him.

The Great Spirit, who was hiding behind a gray cloud in the sky, watched Nasan leave his lodge. The Great Spirit was pleased that his plan had succeeded. He knew that no amount of caution could save Nasan from him once the giant left the protection of the charmed circle.

The moment Nasan stepped across the magic circle, the Great Spirit came out of his hiding place in the sky and seized him. With ten thousand phantom hands the Great Spirit held Nasan. Sharper than spears were the Great Spirit's fingers. Stronger than the bull moose, stronger even than the oak tree, were his hands.

With a roar that echoed across the earth, Nasan tried to break away, but the Great Spirit's hands held the giant on all sides. Like ten thousand hammers the fists of the Great Spirit beat pain against Nasan's bones.

Each way the giant turned and fought, he was beaten back by the phantom hands.

Nasan clutched at the hands he could not see and grappled fiercely with them. But for every hand he tore away from his body, ten more seized him.

The shouts of the Great Spirit and the giant were fearsome to hear, and the earth shook as they struggled with each other.

The fight continued from mountain to plain. Four suns, four moons, the Great Spirit and Nasan the giant fought each other.

Nasan crashed over mountains and staggered backwards into the great broad rivers. The Great Spirit marveled at Nasan's strength. Truly, he was the mightiest of giants.

But the giant fell to the earth at last, exhausted and beaten. The ground shook and crumbled and became a valley where he fell.

Thus, the Great Spirit captured Nasan and pulled him up to the sky.

The Great Spirit was not cruel or wicked, and he admired those who battled bravely and well. The giant, however, had disobeyed the Great Spirit's command, and brave or not, he must be punished.

The Great Spirit changed the giant into a large and awesome eagle.

"Your name shall be Thunderbird, ruler of the thunder and the lightning," the Great Spirit told Nasan. "Once the greatest of all giants, you are now the mightiest of all birds."

The Evening Star Lady was sent back to her place in the sky, and once more there was joy among the Indians.

Around the world Thunderbird now flies, the maker of the storm clouds and a wanderer of the dark skies. His voice is the noise of the thunder and the flash of lightning is the flapping of his wings.

Indian children do not fear the thunder or lightning, not even at night when it awakens them from their sleep. They know it is Nasan the giant, who became the Thunderbird.

OCTOBER

Columbus Day

Columbus Day is celebrated as a holiday throughout North and South America in remembrance of the discovery of the New World on October 12, 1492, by Christopher Columbus. It is right that this man, a great navigator with the courage to undertake the voyage into the unkown, should be so honored.

The first observance of Columbus Day was held in New York City on October 12, 1792, the three hundredth anniversary of the landing. Columbus Day was designated a national holiday just a century later by the Congress of the United States, in 1892.

Christopher Columbus is commemorated not only by the holiday but by the places and institutions named for him, from the District of Columbia, seat of the government of the United States, to the Republic of Colombia in South America; from Mount Columbia in the Rocky Mountains to Columbia University in New York City.

Each year around the twelfth of October, we tell the story of the boy born Cristoforo Colombo in Genoa, Italy, who helped his father, a weaver, at his loom, but longed to go to sea. He read books, particularly those about the travels of Marco Polo, the Venetian, and became a sailor, studying maps and navigation charts. He dreamed of finding a short route to the spices and gold of the Indies.

After work and disappointments, Columbus won the support of King Ferdinand and Queen Isabella of Spain. He was given money, three ships, crewmen, and the title of Admiral of the Ocean Sea. Friar Juan Pérez, a loyal friend, gave his blessing to the flagship, Santa María and the two caravels, Niña and Pinta, as they moved away from Palos, Spain, on August 3, 1492. Columbus and his men sailed westward across the Atlantic and

188

discovered not a short route to Asia but a new world. When the ships at last reached a small island in the Bahamas, Columbus gave it the name San Salvador and offered thanks for a safe voyage. Donning a crimson mantle over his armor, holding the royal banner in his hand, he claimed the land for the rulers of Spain.

In 1492 Columbus did not realize he had discovered land unknown to Europeans. Thinking the islands were part of the Indies, he called the people he met Indians and their territory the West Indies.

Columbus Day is a time to read not only about the voyages of Columbus but also about the Vikings from Scandinavia who some centuries earlier, unknown to Columbus, had explored the northern coast of the new land. It is a time to learn about Amerigo Vespucci, the Italian explorer, for whom the Americas are named.

In many cities, Columbus Day is the occasion for parades and cultural programs.

The Great Discovery

Eleanor Farjeon

Christofero had a mind
Facts were powerless to bind.

He declared that he had seen
Mermaids sporting on the green,

And the world, he used to swear,
Was not an orange, but a pear.

Little wonder then that he,
Blown across the unknown sea

On the quest of far Cathay,
Lit upon the U.S.A.,

And while seeking for the Khan
Met his first Red Indian.

Land! Land in Sight!

Armstrong Sperry

Sunset, on the twenty-fifth of September, found Columbus in his cabin. He was falsifying the record of the day's run. Scarce a cable's length to starboard the *Pinta* was running free before the tradewind; when suddenly a loud cry, winging across the waves, brought the Admiral bounding to his feet.

"*Tierra! Tierra oho!*"

Land! Land in sight!

Even as Columbus raced for the companionway he heard his men burst into a joyous hymn of praise. The crews of the *Pinta* and the *Niña*, too, lifted their voices in thanks to the Almighty. A profound gratitude surged in the Admiral's heart, tightened his throat. High in the rigging, Alfredo shouted that he too could see land—some twenty-five leagues to the southwest.

"Stand by to shorten sail!" cried Columbus. "Bring her round close-hauled on the larboard tack!"

The *Santa María* responded instantly to command. Her sister ships did likewise. In their joy, many sailors flung themselves into the sea, swimming sportively beside the ship.

Darkness shut down. That night men danced and sang on deck. No one closed an eye. No one doubted that morning would see an end to this endless voyage. The wealth of the Indies lay on the horizon!

But by sunrise the vision of land had disappeared, swallowed in the mystery of the sea.

This cruel disappointment plunged all the men into despair. By the public log, the *Santa María* had sailed five hundred and twenty leagues from Ferro. Fortunately, only Columbus knew how far short of the truth this reckoning was. His secret Journal gave the figure at seven hundred and seven leagues!

But ever the ships plowed westward. Birds too small for long-sustained flight came and disappeared at sunset. Fishes were seen of a kind which never swim far from the coast. Branches with fruit still clinging floated on the sluggish tide. The *Niña* signaled that her men had seen a reed and a staff in the water—a small staff which appeared to have been cut with iron. The crew of the *Pinta* reported a branch of thorn with fresh berries on it.

Day and night, with mind and heart intent, all hands searched the horizon in every direction. Each distant cloud took on the shape of land. Every little while, first from one vessel then another, was heard the joyful but false cry: *"Tierra!* Land!"

At seven hundred leagues the Admiral had confidently counted on reaching Cipango. For the first time doubt began to gnaw at his peace of mind. Could he have made some mistake in his calculations? When a large flock of petrels appeared above the ship, he determined that same evening to follow their homeward flight. This decision brought great rejoicing. But though the birds were pursued stubbornly into the west, nothing was seen of land that day, nor the next, nor the one following....

The anxiety of the crew burned like a fever. Something must happen soon. The men had lost faith in signs. Mutiny hung by a trigger balance.

The storm burst when the Admiral scolded the helmsman for allowing the ship to fall off course. Quick as a snake's striking, the sailor's hand darted to his belt. A knife flashed. But Columbus sidestepped the blow. Then he sprang forward, seized the man by his doublet. With a powerful swing he hurled him bodily down the steps. The sailor struck the midships deck with a crash.

Half a dozen of the foremast hands had watched the encounter. Now they raced for the quarterdeck steps, shouting as they ran. Suddenly they halted; for the Admiral had swung an arquebus on its swivel so that it commanded the approach to the poop. They stared into a black and threatening gun muzzle.

"Back, you scum, or I fire!" cried Columbus.

"Hear us, Don Admiral!" a voice shouted defiantly. "Holy Spirit! Would you shoot defenseless men?"

"Since when is a man defenseless with a knife in his hands?" the other flung back. "Say what you want from where you stand. I shoot to kill the first among you who mounts those steps."

It was Alfredo who responded: "They demand that you put about, Don Admiral. Return to Spain——"

A score of voices took up the cry: "Aye! Put about while there's still time. We demand it!"

"You demand?" the Admiral cried scornfully. "Be silent there and listen to me. Before this ship puts about she will reach Cipango. And while one plank of her floats, *I am in command!* Is that clear to you?"

"Admiral," Alfredo protested weakly, "they have made up their minds. Already they have sailed farther than you bargained. They will go no more——"

"Then over the side with them," Columbus thundered. "Let them swim back to Spain. This ship does not put about!"

The gaping threat of the arquebus, the blaze of purpose in the

Admiral's eyes momentarily induced silence. Then one voice whined: "You are carrying us to our death, Admiral. No ship can return against winds that blow ever westward."

"God grant me patience to deal with such an idiot," Columbus ground out. "Don't you know that when a belt of wind blows from one quarter, a similar wind blows from an opposite parallel? God willing, by such a wind we shall return to Spain one day. You have been privileged to travel farther into the Ocean Sea than any man before you. Now you would have me put about and go home to say: 'Let someone else find the way. We failed!' You cowards! Get back to your tasks like men, while still you live."

Once again the Admiral's will prevailed. Scowling but silent, the men returned to their posts. But Columbus knew in his heart that a day would come when words or threats would no longer avail. Before that day, God grant, he would sight land...

Not an eye closed that night. The Admiral took his accustomed stand on the high poop. He ordered the stern lanterns extinguished and with sleepless eyes sought to look into the darkness ahead.

Then, two hours before midnight, the miracle happened. A far-off light struck his eyes. It wavered once or twice, moving quickly on the horizon, like a fisherman's boat rising and falling on the waves. His heart hammered. But he dared not cry out: "*Land!*" He distrusted himself and his senses. He summoned the boatswain.

"Your eyes are sharp, Alfredo," he whispered. "Tell me what you see yonder——" Even as he spoke, the light disappeared.

The boatswain strained into the darkness. "I see nothing, Don Admiral."

The light had reappeared. "Look again!"

"Ah, yes, *yes!* A light. Over there——"

"Quiet! You are certain, Alfredo?"

"But yes, Admiral! It is gone now, yet I saw it, on my oath——"

Surely this was no trick of the eyes! Alfredo had seen it too. Somewhere ahead in darkness were human beings, inhabited land. But so often had hopes been falsely raised, so often dashed, that Columbus commanded Alfredo to keep silent. They stood shoulder to trembling shoulder, staring into the dark.

Hour after hour passed. The sandglass under the helmsman's lantern showed that it was two o'clock in the morning. The hulls of the other two ships loomed vaguely to starboard and in the east the line of the horizon was clearly defined.

Then from the *Pinta* came a flash of flame, a roar of cannon. The long-awaited signal! Land in sight.

Almost instantaneously from the crosstrees came the ringing cry: *"Tierra! Tierra oho!"*

There in the west, green and fair, lay an island.

Who can tell what Christopher Columbus felt at that moment? The long waiting was at an end. The dream had materialized. In his ears rang the voices of his men singing *Te Deum Laudamus*— Almighty God we praise Thee. Voices from the other ships joined in singing the solemn hymn.

Driven by the favoring wind, the three caravels clipped across the equatorial currents, and the hush-hush of their cutwater shattered the morning stillness of the world.

The day was Friday, the twelfth of October, Fourteen Hundred and Ninety-Two.

Veterans Day

OBSERVED ON THE FOURTH MONDAY IN OCTOBER
OBSERVED AS REMEMBRANCE DAY IN CANADA ON NOVEMBER 11

Veterans Day, observed generally in the United States by Presidential proclamation, honors the men and women who have served in the Armed Forces. Veterans Day replaces the earlier holiday, Armistice Day, that each year marked the anniversary of the armistice agreement signed on November 11, 1918, to end World War I. In 1954, Congress changed the name of the celebration to Veterans Day to make this day one that includes veterans of all wars. In Canada, however, November 11 continues to be celebrated as a holiday called Remembrance Day.

When the armistice was signed in Europe in 1918 it meant great rejoicing because four years of war were over. Hope of peace for all time to come was in everyone's heart. But this was not to be, and today we come together to commemorate and give thanks not only to veterans of World War I, but of World War II and the later conflicts fought in Asia. We think of millions of living veterans, and pause to remember those who have died.

For many years, solemn Veterans Day ceremonies have been held in Arlington National Cemetery, across the Potomac River from Washington, D.C. The President or his representative places a wreath at the Tomb of the Unknown Soldier. In cities across the land, there are parades and programs.

On this day we salute the members of the Army, Air Force, Navy, Marines, and Coast Guard. As we do so, we hold the hope that a permanent peace will be achieved among the nations of the earth. Perhaps one step toward such a peace is taken when we become better acquainted with our world neighbors. Reading children's books about the people of other countries contributes to our knowledge and appreciation of each other and the value of world peace.

The Singing Tree

Kate Seredy

This is from the last chapter of the book, The Singing Tree. *The setting is a farm in Hungary during World War I. When his father goes to war, fourteen-year-old Jancsi is left in charge. Homeless relatives, war orphans, and prisoners of war find haven there, hoping for peace between peoples to return.*

"Time goes so fast," Mother sighed one evening in April...April 1918. "The apple tree is showing white; time to thin out my tomato seedlings in the boxes."

"Time...there are so many ways to count the time now," Kate said in a puzzled voice. "Remember, Auntie, when I came to you six years ago, we used to say the same thing: 'Time for the tomato seedlings, the apple tree is showing white.' Later it was time to plant the flower garden because old mother stork was sitting on her eggs. Time for the gypsies was time to dig potatoes in the fall, and when the first snow came it was time to bring out the spinning wheel and the loom for winter evenings.

"Now, I count the time by Daddy's letters. Grigori counts them by sleeps; so do the little children. Hans counts them from the day he...he heard about his father. Uncle Márton, you count them by what the newspapers say about the war, Mari by little Panni's age and teeth, Jancsi by the foals. Grandpa waits for the time when they can go back. Lily...oh, all of us in all different ways. All except you, Auntie. You...oh, I'm all mixed up now..."

She looked around, a little ashamed of this long and slightly incoherent speech. There had been something in her mind she wanted to put into words but with the words coming so slowly the idea had flown.

Uncle Márton was looking at her intently with a very small but very warm smile. They were sitting around the kitchen table, Father, Mother, Grandpa, Grandma, Jancsi, Lily and her Mother, Mari and Kate. The Russians were out in the yard, singing softly to the achy little tune Grigori was playing on his balalaika. The six German children had gone to bed; some with toys, some with forbidden but overlooked kittens (new kittens, all spoken for), and Hans with an ache in his heart that even a kitten could not purr away.

"I don't think you are mixed up, Kate," said Father, still with the warm smile on his face. "I think I know what you were thinking and it's about time somebody put it into words. Let me tell you a story. It will be a war story again. It begins with guns booming and shells screaming, but it will end with the words you were thinking.

"This story began one day in August 1915. We had been advancing all night...all through the long, silent night that followed a day of the heaviest shellfire from both lines, the Russians' and ours. Each had been trying to advance. Finally the Russians left their trenches and retreated. After sundown we were ordered to follow their retreat. We marched or rather crept and crawled and stumbled across this no-man's-land of shell holes, barbed wire, burned-down forests, ruined houses, and deserted Russian gun nests. Except for us, there was nothing alive anywhere. No rabbits scurrying underfoot, no squirrels jumping from tree to tree, no birds, not even an owl hooting, for miles around. Just odds and ends of broken things the war leaves behind.

"All night we crept and crawled and stumbled and still there was only dark night and silence to greet us. Even gunfire would have been welcome in that night, anything to break the spell of having come into a land where only we, creeping men, were alive.

"And then, when men's teeth began to chatter with fear far more benumbing than fear of injury or death, a finger of light, a tiny, weak herald of the approaching dawn, shivered on the edge of darkness, grew less weak, then stronger, changed from gray-green into the palest of yellow streaks across the horizon, turned into gold, then orange, and at last we could see again.

"'Dawn,' a creeping man said as if he had never hoped to see a dawn again.

"Ahead of us and behind us lay a devastated forest with only skeletons of trees still standing here and there. Underfoot there was the same litter of broken things we had come to know by touch, if not by sight...barbed wire, broken guns, empty cartridges, empty tins. All around us was the same silence that had roared in our ears all night.

"And then, as the sun broke through the clouds at last, we saw one tree. One single apple tree that must have been near a house; only the house was no longer there.

"'It is alive,' a creeping man said, but with the words he rose. 'Alive,' another man said as if he never hoped to see a green tree again.

"'It sings,' someone whispered. 'It is alive. I can hear it.'

"Now men rose to their feet and walked and ran like *men*, toward the singing tree, which was alive with birds...living birds singing to the dawn in a live apple tree. Birds. Little wrens and sparrows, late robins, warblers, thrushes, orioles...the green tree was alive with birds all singing...singing to the dawn.

"Against the trunk, owls huddled sleepily; there were jackdaws, and even a crow or two had taken shelter there. Friends and foes of the bird world, side by side, all from different nests, nests that perhaps would never shelter them again, for nests must have fallen with the trees that held them. And here they were, small, feathered orphans of a man-made storm, huddled together on a green apple tree, singing to the dawn.

"Perhaps they too were merely passing time until it would be safe to travel forth and build anew, or seek the old nests. Just passing time, but while they waited, each was singing a song to dawn and each in a different way.

"The one live thing that would never go away unless a man-made gun should uproot it from the earth it grew in was the apple tree. It did not *wait* for time to pass. It did not try to sing. It just *was* what God had made it, a simple, homey tree. Small orphans... large ones...for a while found shelter on its sturdy limbs... They would pass on...."

Father was looking at Mother now and laid his hand on hers folded on the table. "They would pass on. New ones might come. There might be storms again. But she...*she*, mother of all, she would remain the same." He said the last words in a husky voice, looking into Mother's eyes.

The cuckoo clock on the shelf sounded very loud. It had the whole kitchen to itself and made the best of it while human beings kept their silence. Then there was a long, tremulous sigh from Kate that sounded as if she had been holding her breath for too long. Grandpa immediately cleared his throat as only old men can who are very young and soft inside and want to cover it up with a big noise. "Grrrumph! You might as well tell me, Márton...am I the blinking owl or the crow?"

To the little awakening smiles that followed his question, Grandma added a chuckle: "Turning my daughter's head, that's what the man is doing. Never saw the like of him for flowery language. Humph! What's a woman for, if not to take care of those who need her?"

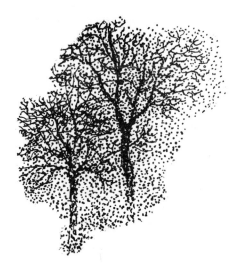

Halloween

Heigh-ho for Halloween!
All the witches to be seen,
Some in black, some in green—
Heigh-ho for Halloween!

English Traditional

The spirit of this old rhyme fits the celebration of Halloween today, a time of fun and frolic especially loved by children. The name Halloween means hallowed, or holy, evening. It was called this because it is the night before All Saints' Day, a Christian holy day more than a thousand years old, celebrated on November first.

Although Halloween takes its name from this Christian festival, most Halloween customs are even older. According to early Celtic beliefs, witches had magic powers on All Hallows' Eve. Ghosts and goblins walked the earth, and mortal men were in close touch with the spirit world. Owls haunted the woods, while cats—sacred cats, black cats, talking cats—prowled in the eerie light of the orange autumn moon.

Coming at summer's end, this was also the feast of fruits, with special attention to apples and nuts. Halloween games such as ducking for apples and telling fortunes with nuts echo long-ago rites that honored the Roman goddess of fruits, Pomona.

Halloween is a favorite time for children's parties at home and school. Pumpkins are changed into grinning jack-o'-lanterns with flickering candles and stare out of windows into the night. Masked goblins, witches, ghosts, and other strange creatures parade the streets of many neighborhoods, calling for treats. It's good fun to read or listen to witching rhymes and spooky stories, some ancient, some new.

October

John Updike

The month is amber,
    Gold, and brown.
Blue ghosts of smoke
    Float through the town,

Great V's of geese
    Honk overhead,
And maples turn
    A fiery red.

Frost bites the lawn.
    The stars are slits
In a black cat's eye
    Before she spits.

At last, small witches,
    Goblins, hags,
And pirates armed
    With paper bags,

Their costumes hinged
    On safety pins,
Go haunt a night
    Of pumpkin grins.

Knurremurre

Ruth Manning-Sanders

There was once a little dwarf man called Katto, and there was once a little dwarf woman called Ulva; and like many a pair of little dwarfs before and after them, Katto and Ulva fell in love with one another. They should have been happy, and they could have been happy, had it not been for Knurremurre. They should have got married, and they would have got married, had it not been that this same Knurremurre fancied the little dwarf woman for himself. And Knurremurre was a terror!

Of all the dwarfs that lived under the hill, he was the strongest; and of all the dwarfs that lived under the hill, he was the richest and the fiercest and the most ill-tempered. In fact, he was a horrible little fellow, and all the other dwarfs were afraid of him.

So when Knurremurre said he was going to marry Ulva himself, what could poor Katto do but bow his head and hide his grief? And what could poor Ulva do? True, she didn't bow her head and hide her grief: she clung to Katto, and threw back her head, and howled long and loud. But that didn't do her any good. Knurre-murre seized her by the hair and dragged her away from Katto, and he got an iron ring and pushed it on her finger, and called all the dwarfs together to witness the marriage ceremony.

"So now you are mine!" he snarled at poor Ulva. "And don't you ever forget it!"

Katto felt that he couldn't stay there under the hill, looking forever at Ulva with longing eyes, and have Ulva forever looking with longing eyes at him. He thought it would be better for them both if he went away. So he changed himself into a fine tortoiseshell cat—perhaps it was his name that gave him the cat idea; at any rate he was a very special-looking cat, with a handsome coat and the most beautiful brown and yellow markings: a cat that anyone would be proud to possess. So he thought he would have no difficulty in finding a good home.

And he did find a good home. He went and rubbed himself against the doorpost of a house belonging to a man called Plat. Plat and his wife were delighted to see him, and they took him in and buttered his paws and gave him a dish of cream. And then he sat in a warm armchair by the stove and purred.

Well, if he could have forgotten Ulva he would have been happy. He had milk and he had bread and he had meat, and he wasn't expected to do anything except look handsome and catch a few mice when he felt inclined. But he couldn't forget Ulva; and so, though he wasn't exactly unhappy, he wasn't exactly happy.

And he lived like that for quite a long time.

Then one morning early, Mr. Plat set out for market. There was nothing unusual about that, because Mr. Plat always had set out for market every Wednesday of his married life. He always set off at eight o'clock in the morning, and he always came back at six o'clock in the evening. And on the Wednesday I'm telling of, he did just that: except that the old clock over the dresser said maybe a few minutes past six when he walked in.

His wife set his supper on the table, and put a saucer of milk on the floor; and Plat sat down at the table, and the tortoiseshell cat jumped out of the armchair, and gave a stretch to his front legs and a stretch to his back legs. And then he settled himself to lap up the milk in his dainty way.

Plat ate a few mouthfuls, and then he put down his knife and fork and laughed.

"I've had a bit of an adventure this evening, that I have," he said.

"Tell about it," said his wife.

And the tortoiseshell cat went on lapping up the milk.

"You ever seen a dwarf?" said Plat.

"No, nor wish to," said the wife.

The tortoiseshell cat stopped lapping the milk for a moment, and lifted up his green eyes to Plat.

"Nor I haven't seen one, neither," said Plat.

"Then why speak of them?" said the wife.

And the tortoiseshell cat went on lapping up the milk.

"I'm coming to that," said Plat. "Now listen, old woman, I was walking across the moor, pleasant as you please, and as I came by a bit of a hill, something hit me on the knee."

"That would be a pebble you kicked up," said the wife.

And the tortoiseshell cat went on lapping up the milk.

"No, it wasn't a pebble I kicked up," said Plat. "It was a pebble thrown at me."

206

"No, not *thrown* at you!" said the wife.

"Yes, thrown at me," said Plat.

And the tortoiseshell cat went on lapping up the milk.

"Who threw it?" said the wife.

"I'm coming to that," said Plat.

"Well then, come to it!" said the wife.

"So I stopped for to rub my knee," said Plat. "And I heard a squeak, squeak, squeaking."

"That would be a bat flickering by in the air," said the wife.

And the tortoiseshell cat went on lapping up the milk.

"No, it wasn't a bat flickering by in the air," said Plat. "It was a voice coming up from the ground."

"No, not a *voice!*" said the wife.

"Yes, a voice," said Plat.

And the tortoiseshell cat lifted his chin from the milk and stared at Plat out of his great green eyes.

"A little bit of a squeaky voice," said Plat, "and it was speaking words."

"No, not *words!*" said the wife.

"Yes, words," said Plat. "I heard 'em plain."

The tortoiseshell cat was still staring at Plat, and Plat stared back and said, "Seems like our puss is listening."

"No, our puss isn't listening," said the wife. "Tell what the voice said; if it was a voice, which I'm not believing."

"It was a voice," said Plat, "and this is what it said,

> *Hark'ee, Plat,*
> *Tell your cat*
> *That Knurremurre's dead.*

Now why should I go for to tell our cat a thing the like of that?"

"It doesn't make sense," said the wife.

It didn't make sense to them, but it made sense to the cat. He jumped up in such a hurry that he overset the saucer of milk. Then he stood on his hind legs and clapped his paws in the air.

"What! Is Knurremurre dead?" he cried in a shrill voice. "Then I may go home as fast as I please!"

And he began to dance around the room and sing,

"Knurremurre is dead! Knurremurre is dead!
So I thank you for board and I thank you for bed,
And Katto and Ulva this night shall be wed."

And with that he gave a leap through the window, and galloped off towards the dwarfs' hill, with his tail sticking up like a flagpole.

Plat stared at his wife, and his wife stared at him.

"Did you ever?" said Plat.

"No, I never did," said his wife.

NOVEMBER

Thanksgiving

The boughs do shake and the bells do ring,
So merrily comes the harvest in,
So merrily comes the harvest in.

We have ploughed, and we have sowed,
We have reaped, and we have mowed,
We have brought home every load,
Hip, hip, hip,
      Harvest Home!

                      Traditional

The spirit of Thanksgiving has long been one of joy. Happiness and gratitude naturally come when it is harvest time, and vegetables, fruit, and grain are safely gathered in.

Celebrating the harvest season is worldwide, and observances go back to ancient times. The Egyptians of long ago gave thanks for well-filled storehouses. The Hindus held a festival for Gauri, goddess of the harvest, and girls wore flowers in their hair. The old Greeks honored Demeter, goddess of agriculture, while Romans celebrated the festival of Ceralia, dedicated to Ceres, goddess of vegetation.

The ancient Hebrews had their Feast of the Tabernacles, or Sukkoth. A harvest booth decorated with sheaves of grain and a pyramid of fruit was a reminder of the exodus from Egypt, when temporary huts offered shelter in the wilderness. American Indians celebrated the harvest by giving thanks to the spirits of the woods for wild game, of the lakes for fish, and of the fields for berries and nuts. At the traditional green corn ceremony, the fires of the old year were put out and new ones kindled.

In America, Thanksgiving is a day set apart to give thanks for the blessings of the year, for food, love, laughter, for freedom and peace to enjoy these gifts. Our celebration probably grew out of the old English festival called harvest home. The first day of thanksgiving in America was held by English colonists in Virginia in 1619.

Thanksgiving, however, is linked more closely with the harvest feast of the Pilgrims of Plymouth in 1621 than with any other. After months of hardship, the Pilgrims had much to be grateful for that first year in a new land. With a plentiful harvest stored away, Governor Bradford set a time for rejoicing and giving thanks. The men brought in seafood and wild turkeys, the women prepared succotash and corn bread. The governor invited Massasoit, Chief of the Wampanoag Indians, whose tribe had befriended the settlers. He came, bringing fifty of his men and a gift of venison. The outdoor feast lasted for three days and included singing, sports, and games.

From that first Pilgrim celebration, the custom of holding a yearly Thanksgiving spread throughout the English Colonies. The first national Thanksgiving proclamation in the young United States was issued by President Washington in November, 1789. The next was proclaimed by President Abraham Lincoln in 1863, and since that time the date has been set each year by Presidential proclamation.

Thanksgiving is celebrated by Canadians at the end of the harvest season, usually in October. The heritage of Thanksgiving in both Canada and the United States is ours to treasure and enjoy.

Prayer for Thanksgiving

Joseph Auslander

We thank thee for our daily bread,
For faith by which the soul is fed,
For burdens given us to bear,
For hope that lifts the heart's despair.

We thank thee, Lord, for eyes to see
The truth that makes, and keeps, men free;
For faults—and for the strength to mend them,
For dreams—and courage to defend them.

We have so much to thank thee for,
Dear Lord, we beg but one boon more;
Peace in the hearts of all men living,
Peace in the whole world this Thanksgiving.

Give My Love to Boston

Elizabeth Coatsworth

"You're late," said the woman gathering apples from the trees along the stone wall as they went by.

"You're late," said the man fishing from the bridge over which they passed.

"You're late," said the farmer who pulled up his team to give them more room.

"You're late," said the old man coming down the steps of the corner store.

"You're late," said the boy driving home the cows from pasture. "The last Thanksgiving turkeys went by a week ago."

It was John who explained, "We got held up. Our father was sick." Molly just listened. The words rang in her ears like a bell, over and over, "You're late, you're late."

Father had said the same thing when they started at dawn.

"You're late getting off. I hope you may get there before snow flies or you're likely to lose some of the flock. But don't drive them too hard for they can't stand it. And take care of yourselves."

Mother had run out with a loaf of bread that she had just pulled out of the oven and put it into the pack Molly carried. John, who was older, had the heavier blankets and the three dollars and sixty-five cents. Grandma stood in the door waving a dishcloth.

"You'll have a beautiful time," she called. "Give my love to Boston."

She didn't say, "You're late." But she was the only one who didn't.

That first day was warm and gentle. There seemed to be no danger in it. John had been to Boston once with Father, but Molly had never been beyond their own valley. When they had climbed the road over the notch and saw all the world spread out below them in brown and gold woodlands and farms set in emerald-green hay stubble cut in squares, and knew that far to the southeast there lay the great city of Boston and the ocean, she could scarcely believe that her own eyes could see so much and so far.

The children went slowly, driving the thirty-four turkeys ahead of them along the grassy edges of the road, so that they might catch crickets and grasshoppers as they went. John took the right hand side and Molly the left and with their long switches ending in tufts of leaves they guided the big birds when they strayed. The turkeys seemed to enjoy themselves. The sun shone along their bronze feathers and the blue and purple-red of the cocks' heads. Most of the time they flowed slowly along like a river and Molly would say to herself, looking at the little brook tumbling head over heels beside the road, "We're all going down hill to Boston." But sometimes the turkeys would be frightened, or try to go into some field by the bars, and then the children had to run to head them off. Old Turk, the leader, tried to help. He had been to Boston three times and knew the road, and the sound of the little bell he wore at his neck steadied the flightier birds. Turk was to come back with them in Samuel Thaxter's wagon after Samuel had unloaded the hams

214

and cheeses he was taking to market.

Sixty miles to go! When a flock started early, they counted on twelve days. But John and Molly were late. It was hard not to urge the turkeys a little. Once or twice when something scared the flock, John let them run for a while instead of trying to head them off and quiet them right away.

"Just that much nearer Boston," he said as Molly, red-faced and panting, joined him.

"But if they scattered, we'd lose a whole lot of time," she said soberly.

"We have to chance it," replied John.

He was fourteen, and nearly as tall as Father now, although his arms and legs still looked too long for him.

Molly was only eight. It was John who was in charge. Molly just helped. John carried the map their father had drawn with the road marked on it and good places to stop for the night where the turkeys could roost in an orchard.

It was fun that first day. They must have done well for they came to the first camping place in good time. The map showed a long stretch of woods beyond, so they didn't try to go farther but asked permission of the farmer to camp in the orchard for the night.

"Sure," said the farmer and his wife said, "You children can bring your blankets in and sleep in the kitchen," but John couldn't leave the flock and Molly wouldn't leave him.

"There's an old haystack at the foot of the orchard," the farmer said then. "You'd better sleep in that."

They ate in the kitchen, however, and the people made them eat with them.

"I know how it is," said the man. "I've taken turkeys to Boston in my time. You young ones are pretty late in getting started, aren't you?"

The hay tickled their faces but it felt warm and soft as they burrowed deep into it. Several times during the night John roused to look at the flock and to make sure that the dark figures roosting among the branches were quiet and safe, but Molly slept all night long, tired after the excitement of the day.

The second day was as beautiful as the first had been, and the turkeys seemed in good humor. John coaxed them along and kept them going almost until dusk, passing the camping place marked on the map and finding another farther down the road. This time they were barely given permission to let their turkeys sleep in the orchard.

"You kids be careful of your fire," the farmer said. "And don't you use any of my fence rails like one crowd did last year."

"And don't pick any apples, either," added his wife. But later she put on her shawl and came down to see how they were getting on.

"I don't know but that you could sleep in the old ice house. It's empty now and the sawdust's dry. And you could keep an eye on your turkeys from there," she said almost grudgingly, and as she turned to go she took two small eggs from the pocket of her apron.

The next day was cloudy and the turkeys seemed to feel the change coming in the air. A colder wind blew, ruffling the bronze of their feathers and the insects were scarcer. The turkey cocks were bad-tempered. They spread their tails and gobbled and teetered on their horny feet as they passed people or dogs along the way. But Turk kept on steadily, his bell ringing, and the children drove the flock along steadily too.

"Might as well get as far as we can while they're fresh," said John.

216

That evening they went on until they came to the fourth camping place on their father's map.

Molly was tired, but she didn't complain. John helped her build the fire in a corner of the stone wall but it kept flattening in the wind and almost going out.

"Here," he said, "put a blanket over your shoulders. I'm going to the store to get some feed."

"But it will cost money," Molly quavered. "We may need it ourselves."

"I got to do the best I can," John explained. "Those turkeys are getting tuckered a little. I got to feed them."

"If only we weren't the last flock."

"Well, we are and it can't be helped."

Molly sat alone for what seemed to her a long time with the turkeys roosted about her in the trees among the low branches. She felt for the first time far away from home and little and lonely. She would have traded Boston and everything in it for a chance to be drying dishes for mother in the lamplit kitchen at home.

When John came back with the feed in a paper bag she felt better.

"He let me have it for a quarter," said John, "and I bought us a new loaf of bread for five cents and five-cents' worth of rock candy, too."

The rock candy made Molly forget her troubles. And they kept the fire going most of the night and weren't very cold either. But the next day it rained and Turk's bell jingled pretty forlornly behind the flock. The turkeys went well enough, helped on with their morning feed of grain, but the road was muddy and both children were wet to the skin. By the time they reached the place marked out for the night they were all glad to stop. It was a drover's inn with a big barnyard and John sent Molly to ask how much it would cost to put the turkeys into the barn for the night.

A white-haired woman opened the door.

"It won't cost you a cent," she said. "But don't tell anyone or my husband wouldn't like it. He's gone to Boston and I can do as I please. Get the turkeys under cover as soon as you can, and come in. I've got a good supper almost ready to serve. Come in and get warm. You look tuckered out."

That night the children ate chicken and dumplings, hot potatoes and spinach and apple pie, and slept in feather beds.

"You'll have one good night's rest if I know it," declared the woman. "And if it's rainy tomorrow, you shan't stir one foot."

"But we're late, Ma'am," said John. "We've got to go on, rain or shine, before the snow catches us."

Fortunately the next morning cleared to the northwest, bright and cold. There was a white frost on the ground but the turkeys didn't seem to mind that, and the freshness in the air put new spirit into their feet as it did for the children. The woman at the inn had fed the flock as well as she had the children and she would take no money.

"All I ask is that you'll stop here again next year," she told them.

All day they travelled well. The road was flattening out now. It was no longer down hill and the farms and villages were closer together. They dreaded the villages where the dogs ran out of the yards to bark at the turkeys and the flock scattered and wasted valuable time. Often kindly passersby would help drive off the dogs and reassemble the birds, but that day they lost their first turkey, a young cock which flew over a couple of fences and disappeared from sight.

"We can't spend half a day chasing him," John decided after an hour's delay. "Father said we'd never get the whole flock there."

The days grew colder, and the nights were so cold that John insisted that Molly must sleep indoors. He paid for her bed and she agreed, knowing that he could have double the number of blankets if she weren't there. They made good time and lost no more turkeys but on the ninth day the air seemed too bright and clear to be trusted.

"It's full moon tonight," said Molly. "Father says look for a change after the full moon."

"If it changes, it won't be for rain," muttered John. "We've only one more day's trip ahead of us, Molly," he said in the late afternoon, "but if it snows tomorrow, maybe we won't be able to get the turkeys through. And if we're delayed for more than a day, we won't have any money left. Do you think you could go on walking by moonlight?"

"I could," said Molly stoutly, "but could the turkeys?"

"We'll have to see."

Before dusk John bought feed and gave the turkeys all they could eat, while he and Molly had a bigger supper than usual by the side of the road. He wrapped her in the blankets and told her to rest until the moon came up and she went to sleep with the turkeys standing uneasily around her.

When she woke up, the fire had gone out and the moon had risen, broad and bright in the sky. John wrapped up the blankets and they started. Old Turk seemed to understand. He drove his turkeys before him down the moonlit road and his bell twinkled like silver in the light. The other turkeys made complaining noises and at first kept stopping but after a while they quieted down and went on. Across the fields now and then they could see the lighted kitchen windows of some farm and all the dogs barked. Once they heard the high yipping of a fox from a pasture ridge and the turkeys huddled and hurried along. The moonlight was so bright that the road showed brown and the grass had a dark green look in the hay-fields, but as the moon rose higher in the sky a wide ring appeared around it white and fleecy, and John said, "The moon's wading in snow."

"There's no star in the ring," said Molly. "That means it'll snow tomorrow."

But in that bright windless night it seemed as though they were walking in a dream. The turkeys moved as in a dream, too, not running from side to side after grasshoppers, but walking quietly along in the middle of the road. The moonlight flowed whitely from their polished feathers and caught on the buckles of the straps across John's shoulders and the ends of Molly's shoe laces. The lights went out in the houses. All the world lay sleeping, but an owl in the woods and a cat hunting along a ditch. Still the turkeys went on and the children followed. When the shadows of the buildings and fences and trees lay almost beneath them and the moon was high overhead and the mist had spread slowly over the sky, John insisted upon a halt.

"But we can go on," Molly argued. "We'd better go on while we're at it."

"No use running a good thing into the ground," declared John. "We're going to eat now, and so're the turkeys. I've got some feed left for them."

"But you don't have to build a fire!"

"Yes, I do. And you're to sit down now and do as you're told."

It was the first time that John had given Molly an order and she obeyed him without further argument.

Once off her feet she thought she'd never get on them again. John wrapped her up and told her to go to sleep but he wouldn't rest himself. He heated water over the fire and made a hot bran for the turkeys and fed them carefully, seeing that the smaller ones got their share. When all had eaten, he stamped out the fire and wakened Molly, who was hard to wake.

"Let me alone," she kept saying, "there's no school today"; but he kept at her until he had roused her at last.

The last half of the night was hard on everyone. Some of the turkeys were limping and the children had to nag at them to keep them going.

"That Turk's a wonder," John said, for he kept driving the flock ahead as steadily as though he had just started. If John's feet were tired, he never showed it any more than Turk did, but Molly was limping and if she hadn't begun to sing hymns, she might have burst out crying. The mist was turning to clouds and the feel of the air had changed. Any country-bred child would have known that snow was coming. The moon was still shining but in a now-you-see-me and now-you-don't way and the ring around the moon looked like a band of copper.

About four in the morning they reached Cousin Jonathan Cole's house in Cambridge and knocked. John knew the house by the red barn with the weathervane of a horse jumping a fence, and the bay window on the right side of a white door with a round knocker, just as Father had said.

Cousin Jonathan came downstairs with a candle and let them in. Then he put on his clothes and helped John get the turkeys under shelter and fed, while Cousin Mattie hurried Molly off to a warm bed.

Neither of the children woke up until noon the next day and it's a wonder that they woke up then, for the light was dimmed by falling snow and the earth was silent under a white blanket already two inches thick.

Perhaps it was the smell of Cousin Mattie's good dinner which wakened them.

"My, you do look more like yourselves," exclaimed Cousin Mattie cheerfully when they appeared washed and dressed at the kitchen door. "You gave me quite a turn last night, like two ghosts."

"I'd better go see to the turkeys," said John but Cousin Mattie smiled and shook her head. "Jonathan drove into the market with them this morning in the big cart," she explained. "He's just back and gone out to put up the horses. He got a good price for the turkeys on a late market."

"But he didn't take Turk?" asked Molly anxiously.

"No, he understood about Turk. Turk's out at the barn, now, swelling about, proud of the trip he's made. And well he may be! No one's ever made such good time with a flock to our knowledge, and they brought a better price than they would have last week when the market was full of turkeys. Folks don't think Thanksgiving's Thanksgiving without a turkey on the platter, but there's a lot will leave it till the last minute. Here's your Cousin Jonathan. You'd better all eat a good dinner, for you've lots to do and see before Samuel Thaxter stops to pick you up on Monday morning."

DECEMBER

Hanukkah

OBSERVED EIGHT DAYS COMMENCING ON THE TWENTY-FIFTH DAY
OF THE HEBREW MONTH OF KISLEV, USUALLY IN DECEMBER

Hanukkah is a family festival, one of the brightest in the Jewish calendar. Hanukkah is the Feast of Dedication, also called the Festival of Lights.

The Hebrew word "hanukkah" means dedication, and this season recalls an important event in Jewish history, the rededication of the Temple of Jerusalem after the victory of the Jews. Led by Judah Maccabaeus, they had defeated the Syrian king, Antiochus IV. A period of living as a conquered people was ended. When the Temple was restored, the people wished to rekindle the light that had burned there. But the oil was only enough for one day—and still the light burned for eight days. Thus the Hanukkah season lasts for eight days, with a new candle lighted symbolically on each day.

A special ceremony surrounds lighting the first candle. As the family watches, the father brings the "helping candle," the shamash, close to the wick of the first of the candles in the branched candleholder called the menorah. Blessings are said, and traditional songs are sung. On each of the next seven days another candle is lighted.

Hanukkah is a joyous holiday, celebrated as a religious festival and a family feast. Much attention centers around the children in the home, and grandparents and other relatives take part. A four-sided top called a dreydel is a traditional part of the fun. Four letters of the Hebrew alphabet appear on the sides of the top, N, G, H, and Sh. There are special foods and often gifts, sometimes one to open on each of the eight days. Joy mixes with the serious meaning of this holiday as the days pass by all too quickly.

Zlateh the Goat

*Isaac Bashevis Singer translated
by the Author and Elizabeth Shub*

At Hanukkah time the road from the village to the town is usually covered with snow, but this year the winter had been a mild one. Hanukkah had almost come, yet little snow had fallen. The sun shone most of the time. The peasants complained that because of the dry weather there would be a poor harvest of winter grain. New grass sprouted, and the peasants sent their cattle out to pasture.

For Reuven the furrier it was a bad year, and after long hesitation he decided to sell Zlateh the goat. She was old and gave little milk. Feyvel the town butcher had offered eight gulden for her. Such a sum would buy Hanukkah candles, potatoes and oil for pancakes, gifts for the children, and other holiday necessaries for the house. Reuven told his oldest boy Aaron to take the goat to town.

Aaron understood what taking the goat to Feyvel meant, but he had to obey his father. Leah, his mother, wiped the tears from her eyes when she heard the news. Aaron's younger sisters, Anna and Miriam, cried loudly. Aaron put on his quilted jacket and a cap with earmuffs, bound a rope around Zlateh's neck, and took along two slices of bread with cheese to eat on the road. Aaron was supposed to deliver the goat by evening, spend the night at the butcher's, and return the next day with the money.

While the family said good-bye to the goat, and Aaron placed the rope around her neck, Zlateh stood as patiently and good-naturedly as ever. She licked Reuven's hand. She shook her small white beard. Zlateh trusted human beings. She knew that they always fed her and never did her any harm.

When Aaron brought her out on the road to town, she seemed somewhat astonished. She'd never been led in that direction before. She looked back at him questioningly, as if to say, "Where are you taking me?" But after a while she seemed to come to the conclusion that a goat shouldn't ask questions. Still, the road was different. They passed new fields, pastures, and huts with thatched roofs. Here and there a dog barked and came running after them, but Aaron chased it away with his stick.

The sun was shining when Aaron left the village. Suddenly the weather changed. A large black cloud with a bluish center appeared in the east and spread itself rapidly over the sky. A cold wind blew in with it. The crows flew low, croaking. At first it looked as if it would rain, but instead it began to hail as in summer. It was early in the day, but it became dark as dusk. After a while the hail turned to snow.

In his twelve years Aaron had seen all kinds of weather, but he had never experienced a snow like this one. It was so dense it shut out the light of the day. In a short time their path was completely covered. The wind became as cold as ice. The road to town was narrow and winding. Aaron no longer knew where he was. He could not see through the snow. The cold soon penetrated his quilted jacket.

At first Zlateh didn't seem to mind the change in weather. She too was twelve years old and knew what winter meant. But when her legs sank deeper and deeper into the snow, she began to turn her head and look at Aaron in wonderment. Her mild eyes seemed to ask, "Why are we out in such a storm?" Aaron hoped that a peasant would come along with his cart, but no one passed by.

The snow grew thicker, falling to the ground in large, whirling flakes. Beneath it Aaron's boots touched the softness of a plowed field. He realized that he was no longer on the road. He had gone astray. He could no longer figure out which was east or west, which way was the village, the town. The wind whistled, howled, whirled the snow about in eddies. It looked as if white imps were playing tag on the fields. A white dust rose above the ground. Zlateh stopped. She could walk no longer. Stubbornly she anchored her cleft hooves in the earth and bleated as if pleading to be taken home. Icicles hung from her white beard, and her horns were glazed with frost.

Aaron did not want to admit the danger, but he knew just the same that if they did not find shelter they would freeze to death. This was no ordinary storm. It was a mighty blizzard. The snowfall had reached his knees. His hands were numb, and he could no longer feel his toes. He choked when he breathed. His nose felt like wood, and he rubbed it with snow. Zlateh's bleating began to sound like crying. Those humans in whom she had so much confidence had dragged her into a trap. Aaron began to pray to God for himself and for the innocent animal.

Suddenly he made out the shape of a hill. He wondered what it could be. Who had piled snow into such a huge heap? He moved toward it, dragging Zlateh after him. When he came near it, he

227

realized that it was a large haystack which the snow had blanketed.

Aaron realized immediately that they were saved. With great effort he dug his way through the snow. He was a village boy and knew what to do. When he reached the hay, he hollowed out a nest for himself and the goat. No matter how cold it may be outside, in the hay it is always warm. And hay was food for Zlateh. The moment she smelled it she became contented and began to eat. Outside the snow continued to fall. It quickly covered the passageway Aaron had dug. But a boy and an animal need to breathe, and there was hardly any air in their hideout. Aaron bored a kind of a window through the hay and snow and carefully kept the passage clear.

Zlateh, having eaten her fill, sat down on her hind legs and seemed to have regained her confidence in man. Aaron ate his two slices of bread and cheese, but after the difficult journey he was still hungry. He looked at Zlateh and noticed her udders were full. He lay down next to her, placing himself so that when he milked her he could squirt the milk into his mouth. It was rich and sweet. Zlateh was not accustomed to being milked that way, but she did not resist. On the contrary, she seemed eager to reward Aaron for bringing her to a shelter whose very walls, floor, and ceiling were made of food.

Through the window Aaron could catch a glimpse of the chaos outside. The wind carried before it whole drifts of snow. It was completely dark, and he did not know whether night had already come or whether it was the darkness of the storm. Thank God that in the hay it was not cold. The dried hay, grass, and field flowers exuded the warmth of the summer sun. Zlateh ate frequently; she nibbled from above, below, from the left and right. Her body gave forth an animal warmth, and Aaron cuddled up to her. He had always loved Zlateh, but now she was like a sister. He was alone, cut off from his family, and wanted to talk. He began to talk to Zlateh. "Zlateh, what do you think about what has happened to us?" he asked.

"Maaaa," Zlateh answered.

"If we hadn't found this stack of hay, we would both be frozen stiff by now," Aaron said.

"Maaaa," was the goat's reply.

"If the snow keeps on falling like this, we may have to stay here for days," Aaron explained.

"Maaaa," Zlateh bleated.

"What does 'Maaaa' mean?" Aaron asked. "You'd better speak up clearly."

"Maaaa. Maaaa," Zlateh tried.

"Well, let it be 'Maaaa' then," Aaron said patiently. "You can't speak, but I know you understand. I need you and you need me. Isn't that right?"

"Maaaa."

Aaron became sleepy. He made a pillow out of some hay, leaned his head on it, and dozed off. Zlateh too fell asleep.

When Aaron opened his eyes, he didn't know whether it was morning or night. The snow had blocked up his window. He tried to clear it, but when he had bored through to the length of his arm, he still hadn't reached the outside. Luckily he had his stick with him and was able to break through to the open air. It was still dark outside. The snow continued to fall and the wind wailed, first with one voice and then with many. Sometimes it had the sound of devilish laughter. Zlateh too awoke, and when Aaron greeted her, she answered, "Maaaa." Yes, Zlateh's language consisted of only one word, but it meant many things. Now she was saying, "We must accept all that God gives us—heat, cold, hunger, satisfaction, light, and darkness."

Aaron had awakened hungry. He had eaten up his food, but Zlateh had plenty of milk.

For three days Aaron and Zlateh stayed in the haystack. Aaron had always loved Zlateh, but in these three days he loved her more and more. She fed him with her milk and helped him keep warm. She comforted him with her patience. He told her many stories, and she always cocked her ears and listened. When he patted her, she licked his hand and his face. Then she said, "Maaaa," and he knew it meant, I love you too.

The snow fell for three days, though after the first day it was not as thick and the wind quieted down. Sometimes Aaron felt that there could never have been a summer, that the snow had always fallen, ever since he could remember. He, Aaron, never had a father or mother or sisters. He was a snow child, born of the snow, and so was Zlateh. It was so quiet in the hay that his ears rang in the stillness. Aaron and Zlateh slept all night and a good part of the day. As for Aaron's dreams, they were all about warm weather. He dreamed of green fields, trees covered with blossoms, clear brooks, and singing birds. By the third night the snow had stopped, but Aaron did not dare to find his way home in the darkness. The sky became clear and the moon shone, casting silvery nets on the snow. Aaron dug his way out and looked at the world. It was all white, quiet, dreaming dreams of heavenly splendor. The stars were large and close. The moon swam in the sky as in a sea.

On the morning of the fourth day Aaron heard the ringing of

sleigh bells. The haystack was not far from the road. The peasant who drove the sleigh pointed out the way to him — not to the town and Feyvel the butcher, but home to the village. Aaron had decided in the haystack that he would never part with Zlateh.

Aaron's family and their neighbors had searched for the boy and the goat but had found no trace of them during the storm. They feared they were lost. Aaron's mother and sisters cried for him; his father remained silent and gloomy. Suddenly one of the neighbors came running to their house with the news that Aaron and Zlateh were coming up the road.

There was great joy in the family. Aaron told them how he had found the stack of hay and how Zlateh had fed him with her milk. Aaron's sisters kissed and hugged Zlateh and gave her a special treat of chopped carrots and potato peels, which Zlateh gobbled up hungrily.

Nobody ever again thought of selling Zlateh, and now that the cold weather had finally set in, the villagers needed the services of Reuven the furrier once more. When Hanukkah came, Aaron's mother was able to fry pancakes every evening, and Zlateh got her portion too. Even though Zlateh had her own pen, she often came to the kitchen, knocking on the door with her horns to indicate that she was ready to visit, and she was always admitted. In the evening Aaron, Miriam, and Anna played dreidel. Zlateh sat near the stove watching the children and the flickering of the Hanukkah candles.

Once in a while Aaron would ask her, "Zlateh, do you remember the three days we spent together?"

And Zlateh would scratch her neck with a horn, shake her white bearded head and come out with the single sound which expressed all her thoughts, and all her love.

Christmas

OBSERVED ON DECEMBER 25

Around the world, Christmas is one of the most joyful days of the year. Among Christians, the day honors the birth of the Christ Child. But whether the observance of the holiday is sacred or secular, Christmas is essentially a family festival whose spirit is best expressed in the happiness of children.

The Christmas story, beautiful in its simplicity, is narrated in the Gospels of Matthew and Luke in the New Testament. It is a tale of wonder: a star in the sky, an angel's song, shepherds in the field, the Child in the manger, and the Three Wise Men from the East offering precious gifts.

The marvel, mystery, and human tenderness of the Christmas story have inspired people for centuries. Artists, poets, storytellers, and musicians have woven its spell into paintings and stained glass, folklore, carols, and the legends of many countries.

This is a season of happy tradition, and our celebrations reflect some of the best-loved customs of many nations. In America, Christmas is a time of giving and sharing, bell ringing and carol singing, church going, hospitality, and festive foods.

Candles brighten homes, and Christmas trees sparkle with firefly lights and glittering ornaments. Rooms are decorated with berried garlands and greens. Cards from near and far strengthen ties of love and memory.

There are bowls of nuts and apples, and perhaps strings of popcorn and cookie ornaments to hang on the Christmas tree. There are delicious breads and cakes from the recipes of cooks around the world. Italian panettone, German stollen, the French cake of the Kings, the honey lebkuchen of the Pennsylvania Dutch add to the pleasure of the feast.

In the United States and Canada, and in other countries as

well, Santa Claus is given credit for filling the stockings hung by the fireplace or at the foot of the bed. Spanish children believe the Three Kings bring gifts found in straw-filled shoes, while Dutch and Belgian children have earlier welcomed Saint Nicholas on his day, December 6. In Sweden, the lovely Saint Lucia customs commence the holiday season.

Ornaments of straw and colored yarn are made in Lithuania and the Scandinavian countries. Beautifully carved nativity figures are the work of folk artists in many European countries. The yule log, whose history goes back to pre-Christian times, is burned on hearths in England and France. Children in Mexico shatter the piñata to enjoy a shower of candies and small gifts.

The Christmas season is a time for books, too, and for reading stories and poems which make the holiday richer. There is a folk belief that nature as well as man honors the birth of Christ and that at midnight on Christmas Eve animals speak, bees hum, and roosters crow. Poets from Shakespeare to Thomas Hardy and Phyllis McGinley have turned such legends into literature. Attracted to the part played by birds in the celebration, poets and singers have fashioned rhymes about the robin, the wren, and the partridge in the pear tree. There are stories, too, about flowers and plants. The Christmas rose is one such flower, and another is the flaming poinsettia, called the "flower of the Holy Night" in Mexico.

Clement Moore gave us the jolly, white-bearded and red-cloaked Santa who rides his reindeer-drawn sleigh through the sky in "The Night Before Christmas." Hans Christian Andersen in Denmark, Charles Dickens in England, and Dylan Thomas in Wales, each wrote in his own way about memorable Christmases. Authors of today continue this tradition, linking country to country, generation to generation, in friendship and peace—and so we say "Merry Christmas, and good reading to all!"

Now Every Child

Eleanor Farjeon

Now every Child that dwells on earth,
    Stand up, stand up and sing!
The passing night has given birth
    Unto the Children's King.
        Sing sweet as the flute,
        Sing clear as the horn,
        Sing joy of the Children
        Come Christmas the morn!
        Little Christ Jesus
        Our Brother is born.

Schnitzle, Schnotzle, and Schnootzle

Ruth Sawyer

The Tirol straddles the Alps and reaches one hand into Italy and another into Austria. There are more mountains in the Tirol than you can count, and every Alp has its story.

Long ago, some say on the Brenner-Alp, some say on the Mitterwald-Alp, there lived the king of all the goblins of the Tirol, and his name was Laurin. King Laurin. His kingdom was under the earth, and all the gold and silver of the mountains he owned. He had a daughter, very young and very lovely, not at all like her father, who had a bulbous nose, big ears, and a squat figure, and looked as old as the mountains. She loved flowers and was sad that none grew inside her father's kingdom.

"I want a garden of roses—red roses, pink roses, blush roses, flame roses, shell roses, roses like the sunrise and the sunset." This she said one day to her father. And the king laughed and said she should have just such a garden. They would roof it with crystal, so that the sun would pour into the depths of the kingdom and make the roses grow lovely and fragrant. The garden was planted and every rare and exquisite rose bloomed in it. And so much color they spread upwards on the mountains around that the snow caught it and the mortals living in the valley pointed at it with wonder. "What is it makes our Alps so rosy, so glowing?" they asked. And they spoke of it ever after as the alpen-glow.

I have told you this that you might know what kind of goblin King Laurin was. He was merry, and he liked to play pranks and have fun. He liked to go abroad into the valleys where the mortals lived, or pop into a herdsman's hut halfway up the mountain. There were men who said they had seen him — that small squat figure with a bulbous nose and big ears — gamboling with the goats on a summer day. And now I begin my story. It is an old one that Tirolese mothers like to tell their children.

Long ago there lived in one of the valleys a very poor cobbler indeed. His wife had died and left him with three children, little boys, all of them — Fritzl, Franzl, and Hansl. They lived in a hut so small there was only one room in it, and in that was the cobbler's bench, a hearth for cooking, a big bed full of straw, and on the wall racks for a few dishes, and, of course, there was a table with a settle and some stools. They needed few dishes or pans, for there was never much to cook or eat. Sometimes the cobbler would mend the Sunday shoes of a farmer, and then there was good goats' milk to drink. Sometimes he would mend the holiday shoes of the baker, and then there was the good long crusty loaf of bread to eat. And sometimes he mended the shoes of the butcher, and then there was the good stew, cooked with meat in the pot, and noodles, leeks, and herbs. When the cobbler gathered the little boys around the table and they had said their grace, he would laugh and clap his hands and sometimes even dance. "Ha-ha!" he would shout. "Today we have the good...what? Ah-h...today we eat...Schnitzle, Schnotzle, and Schnootzle!"

With that he would swing the kettle off the hook and fill every bowl brimming full, and Fritzl, Franzl, and Hansl would eat until they had had enough. Ach, those were the good days — the days of having Schnitzle, Schnotzle, and Schnootzle. Of course, the cobbler was making up nonsense and nothing else, but the stew tasted so much better because of the nonsense.

Now a year came, with every month following his brother on leaden feet. The little boys and the cobbler heard the month of March tramp out and April tramp in. They heard June tramp out and July tramp in. And every month marched heavier than his brother. And that was because war was among them again. War, with workers taking up their guns and leaving mothers and children to care for themselves as best they could; and there was scant to pay even a poor cobbler for mending shoes. The whole village shuffled to church with the soles flapping and the heels lopsided, and the eyelets and buttons and straps quite gone.

Summer — that was not so bad. But winter came and covered up the good earth, and gone were the roots, the berries, the sorrel, and the corn. The tramp of November going out and December coming in was very loud indeed. The little boys were quite sure that the two months shook the hut as they passed each other on the mountainside.

As Christmas grew near, the little boys began to wonder if there would be any feast for them, if there would be the good father dancing about the room and laughing "Ha-ha," and singing "Ho-ho," and saying: "Now, this being Christmas Day we have the good... what?" And this time the little boys knew that they would never wait for their father to say it; they would shout themselves: "We know — it is the good Schnitzle, Schnotzle, and Schnootzle!" Ach, how very long it was since their father had mended shoes for the butcher! Surely — surely — there would be need soon again, with Christmas so near.

At last came the Eve of Christmas. The little boys climbed along the beginnings of the Brenner-Alp, looking for fagots. The trees had shed so little that year; every branch was green and grew fast to its tree, so few twigs had snapped, so little was there of dead, dried brush to fill their arms.

Their father came in when they had a small fire started, blowing his whiskers free of icicles, slapping his arms about his big body, trying to put warmth back into it. "Na-na, nobody will have a shoe mended today. I have asked everyone. Still there is good news. The soldiers are marching into the village. The inn is full. They will have boots that need mending, those soldiers. You will see." He pinched a cheek of each little boy; he winked at them and nodded his head. "You shall see — tonight I will come home with...what?"

"Schnitzle, Schnotzle, and Schnootzle," they shouted together, those three.

So happy they were they forgot there was nothing to eat for supper — not a crust, not a slice of cold porridge-pudding, not the smallest sup of goats' milk. "Will the soldiers have money to pay you?" asked Fritzl, the oldest.

"Not the soldiers, perhaps, but the captains. There might even be a general. I will mend the boots of the soldiers for nothing, for after all what day is coming tomorrow! They fight for us, those soldiers; we mend for them, ja? But a general — he will have plenty of money."

The boys stood about while their father put all his tools, all his pieces of leather into a rucksack; while he wound and wound and wound the woolen scarf about his neck, while he pulled the cap far down on his head. "It will be a night to freeze the ears off you," he said. "Now bolt the door after me, keep the fire burning with a little at a time; and climb into the straw-bed and pull the quilt over you. And let no one in!"

He was gone. They bolted the door; they put a little on the fire; they climbed into the big bed, putting Hansl, the smallest, in the middle. They pulled up the quilt, such a thin quilt to keep out so much cold! Straight and still and close together they lay, looking up at the little spot of light the fire made on the ceiling, watching their breath go upwards in icy spurts. With the going of the sun the wind rose. First it whispered: it whispered of good fires in big chimneys; it whispered of the pines on the mountainsides; it whispered of snow loosening and sliding over the glaciers. Then it began to blow: it blew hard, it blew quarrelsome, it blew cold and colder. And at last it roared. It roared its wintry breath through the cracks in the walls and under the door. And Fritzl, Franzl, and Hansl drew closer together and shivered.

"Whee...ooh...bang, bang! Whee...ooh...bang, bang!"

"Is it the wind or someone knocking?" asked Franzl.

"It is the wind," said Fritzl.

"Whee...ooh...knock, knock!"

"Is it the wind or someone knocking?" asked Hansl.

"It is the wind *and* someone knocking!" said Fritzl.

He rolled out of the bed and went to the window. It looked out directly on the path to the door. "Remember what our father said: do not open it," said Franzl.

But Fritzl looked and looked. Close to the hut, beaten against it by the wind, stood a little man no bigger than Hansl. He was pounding on the door. Now they could hear him calling: "Let me in! I tell you, let me in!"

"Oh, don't, don't!" cried Hansl.

"I must," said Fritzl. "He looks very cold. The wind is tearing at him as a wolf tears at a young lamb"; and with that he drew the bolt and into the hut skipped the oddest little man they had ever seen. He had a great peaked cap tied onto his head with deer-thongs. He had a round red face out of which stuck a bulbous nose, like a fat plum on a pudding. He had big ears. And his teeth were chattering so hard they made the stools to dance. He shook his fist at the three little boys. "Ach, kept me waiting. Wanted to keep all the good food, all the good fire to yourselves? Na-na, that is no kind of hospitality."

He looked over at the little bit of a fire on the hearth, making hardly any heat in the hut. He looked at the empty table, not a bowl set or a spoon beside it. He took up the big pot, peered into it, turned it upside down to make sure nothing was clinging to the bottom, set it down with a bang. "So — you have already eaten it all. Greedy boys. But if you have saved no feast for me, you can at least warm me." With that he climbed into the big straw-bed with Franzl and Hansl, with his cap still tied under his chin. Fritzl tried to explain that they had not been greedy, that there had never been any food, not for days, to speak of. But he was too frightened of the little man, of his eyes as sharp and blue as ice, of his mouth so grumbling.

"Roll over, roll over," the little man was shouting at the two in the bed. "Can't you see I have no room? Roll over and give me my half of the quilt."

Fritzl saw that he was pushing his brothers out of the bed. "Na-na," he said, trying to make peace with their guest. "They are little, those two. There is room for all if we but lie quiet." And he started to climb into the bed himself, pulling gently at the quilt that there might be a corner for him.

But the little man bounced and rolled about shouting: "Give me room, give me more quilt. Can't you see I'm cold? I call this poor hospitality to bring a stranger inside your door, give him nothing to eat, and then grudge him bed and covering to keep him warm." He dug his elbow into the side of skinny little Hansl.

"Ouch!" cried the boy.

Fritzl began to feel angry. "Sir," he said, "sir, I pray you to be gentle with my little brother. And I am sorry there has been nothing to give you. But our father, the cobbler, has gone to mend shoes for the soldiers. When he returns we look for food. Truly, this is a night to feast and to share. So if you will but lie still until he comes I can promise you..."

The little man rolled over and stuck his elbow into Fritzl's ribs. "Promise—promise. Na-na, what good is a promise? Come get out of bed and give me your place." He drew up his knees, put his feet in the middle of Fritzl's back and pushed with a great strength. The next moment the boy was spinning across the room. "There you go," roared the little man after him. "If you must keep warm turn cartwheels, turn them fast."

For a moment Fritzl stood sullenly by the small speck of fire. He felt bruised and very angry. He looked over at the bed. Sure enough, the greedy little man had rolled himself up in the quilt leaving only a short corner of it for the two younger boys. He had taken more than half of the straw for himself, and was even then pushing and digging at Hansl. He saw Franzl raise himself up and take the place of his littlest brother, that he should get the digs.

Brrr...it was cold! Before he knew it Fritzl was doing as he had been told, turning cartwheels around the room. He had rounded the table and was coming toward the bed when — plop! Plop — plop — plop! Things were falling out of his pockets every time his feet swung high over his head. Plop — plop — plop! The two younger boys were sitting up in bed. It was their cries of astonishment which brought Fritzl's feet back to the floor again, to stay. In a circle about the room, he had left behind him a golden trail of oranges. Such oranges — big as two fists! And sprinkled everywhere between were comfits wrapped in gold and silver paper. Fritzl stood and gaped at them.

"Here, you, get out and keep warm yourself!" shouted the little man as he dug Franzl in the ribs. "Cartwheels for you, boy!" And the next minute Franzl was whirling in cartwheels about the room. Plop — plop — plop — things were dropping out of his pockets: Christmas buns, Christmas cookies covered with icing, with plums, with anise and caraway seeds.

The little man was digging Hansl now in the ribs. "Lazy boy, greedy boy. Think you can` have the bed to yourself now? Na-na, I'll have it! Out you go!" And he put his feet against the littlest boy's back and pushed him onto the floor. "Cartwheels..." he began; but

Fritzl, forgetting his amazement at what was happening, shouted: "But, sir, he is too little. He cannot turn..."

"Hold him up in the corner, then. You keep warmer when your heels are higher than your head. Step lively there. Take a leg, each of you, and be quick about it."

So angry did the little man seem, so fiery and determined, that Fritzl and Franzl hurried their little brother over to the chimney corner, stood him on his head and each held a leg. Donner and Blitzen! What happened then! Whack — whack — whickety-whack! Whack — whack — whickety-whack! Pelting the floor like hail against the roof came silver and gold pieces, all pouring out of Hansl's pockets.

Fritzl began to shout, Franzl began to dance. Hansl began to shout: "Let me down, let me down!" When they did the three little boys danced around the pile, taking hands, singing "Tra-la-la," and "Fiddle-de-dee," and "Ting-a-ling-a-ling," until their breath was gone and they could dance no longer. They looked over at the bed and Fritzl was opening his mouth to say: "Now, if you please, sir, we can offer you some Christmas cheer..." But the bed was empty, the quilt lay in a heap on the floor. The little man had gone.

The three little boys were gathering up the things on the floor — putting oranges into the big wooden bowl, buns and cookies onto the two platters, silver and gold pieces into this dish and that. And right in the midst of it in came their father, stamping, puffing in through the door. He had brought bread, he had brought milk, he had brought meat for the good stew — and noodles.

Such a wonder, such a clapping of hands, such a singing as they worked to get ready the Christmas feast! Fritzl began the story about their Christmas guest; Franzl told it midthrough; but little Hansl finished, making his brothers stand him in the corner again on his head to show just how it was that all the silver and gold had tumbled out of his pockets.

"Na-na," said the cobbler, "we are the lucky ones. I did not know it was true; always I thought it was a tale the grandfathers told the children. The saying goes that King Laurin comes every year at the Christmas to one hut—one family—to play his tricks and share his treasure horde."

"He was a very ugly little man," said Hansl. "He dug us in our ribs and took all the bed for himself."

"That was the king—that is the way he plays at being fierce. Say: '*Komm, Herr Jesus, und sei unser Gast,*' then draw up the stools. Ah-h...what have we to eat?"

The little boys shouted the answer all together: "Schnitzle—Schnotzle—and Schnootzle!"

Watch

Juan Ramón Jiménez,
translated by Eloise Roach

The lamb baaed gently.
The tender donkey showed its joy
in lusty bray.
The dog barked playfully
almost talking to the stars.

I could not sleep. I went outdoors
and saw heavenly tracks upon the ground
all flower-decked
like a sky
turned upside down.

A warm and fragrant mist
hovered over the grove;
the moon was sinking low
in a soft golden west
of divine orbit.

My breast beat without pause,
as if my heart had wined...

I opened wide the stable door to see
if He were there.
        He was!

Carol of the Brown King

Langston Hughes

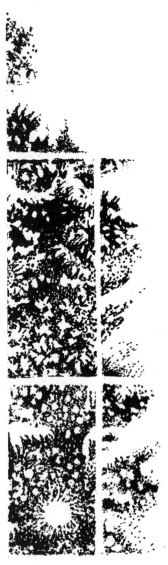

Of the three Wise Men
Who came to the King,
One was a brown man,
So they sing.

Of the three Wise Men
Who followed the Star,
One was a brown king
From afar.

They brought fine gifts
Of spices and gold
In jeweled boxes
Of beauty untold.

Unto His humble
Manger they came
And bowed their heads
In Jesus' name.

Three Wise Men,
One dark like me —
Part of His
Nativity.

The Three Magi

Pura Belpré

It was the fifth of January, the eve of the Three Kings' Day, the day when all Spanish children eagerly await their Christmas presents. In the sumptuous Palace of the Orient, where the Magi Kings lived, reigned great excitement and confusion. The royal doorman had been busy all morning answering the bell as the couriers came from the four corners of the world, bringing the royal mail. Inside the palace the Lord Chamberlain's voice could be heard giving orders to his hundred servants.

"Open the windows!" he shouted, and a hundred men, glittering in uniforms decked with gold and silver in which the initials "M.M." (Magi Messengers) stood out, ran from one side of the spacious hall to the other and opened wide the royal windows, letting in the cool air.

"Kerchoo! Kerchoo!" sneezed the Chamberlain.

"Bring my highest powdered wig," he called.

Again the hundred servants darted on, getting in each other's way, stumbling over chairs and sofas, until finally a very tall and thin one was able to free himself from the rest and bring out an immense wig, which he placed on the Chamberlain's head.

In the royal kitchen the noise rose like a thunderous wave. Like a captain before his army and clad in white apron and high cap the royal chef stood. With hands folded across his voluminous stomach, he gravely directed his men. They carried out his orders with dexterity and care.

At his signal, eggs were broken and beaten to soft fluffy foam, flour kneaded and almonds and nuts grated to a fine powder. From the oven and frying pans rose the smell of sweetmeats and roasts. It was evident that in the royal kitchen of the Three Magi, the innumerable cooks were getting ready an immense repast for a long journey.

Outside the palace in the royal stables, the stamping and neighing of the royal horses could be heard for miles around. Lines and lines of coaches, covered with heavy blankets, could be seen down the hall.

"There comes Carlos again," whispered a dapple gray horse to another.

"Stop your stamping, stop it this minute," called out Carlos, as he opened the door.

In reply, the horses raised their heads and neighed loudly and resonantly.

"I know, I know," said Carlos, "but this is the eve of the Three Kings' Day, and it's the camels the Magi want and not horses. Stop your neighing. Stop your stamping."

Slowly he opened the door and led the camels to the public square. Already people were gathered there, while the stable hands brought gallons of water, baskets of scented soaps, and a great number of combs and brushes.

The royal camels were about to receive their bath and this was a ceremony always performed in public. First, the water was poured reverently over their backs. Then the stable boys divided into groups of ten and, armed with soap and brushes, began the scrubbing. This finished, another group would begin the combing and smoothing of the hair. Decked then with red mantles and silver reins, the three choice stable boys, Carlos, Juan, and Pedro led them to the door of the royal palace. Three magnificent-looking camels of the Three Magi were the happiest camels in the entire world, for it was the fifth of January and they were to carry on their backs the three most wished-for persons in the children's world—King Gaspar, King Melchor, and King Baltazar. But they were impatient as they stood there. Putting their three heads together, they asked each other: "Where are the Three Magi? Why do they keep us waiting?"

And well might they ask, for the Three Kings could hardly be seen at that time.

In the Grand Throne Room, behind a barricade of opened envelopes, they sat, laughing and nodding at each other as they read and carefully put away millions of letters sent them. There were letters of all sizes and colors. Some of them were written on new paper with gilt borders, others embellished with flowers and birds, written in clear and legible handwriting, but the majority of them—and these were the ones the Kings liked best—were written on scraps of paper, and full of blots of ink and many erasures. They all carried the same message—a plea for some particular toy and a promise to be a better boy or girl in the future.

Finally, the last letter was read and carefully put away. Slowly the Three Magi rose from their beautiful thrones and left the room. The royal doorman saw them coming and opened the door widely. Solemn in their approach, majestic in their bearing, handsomely garbed with precious stones and jewelry, and with their ermine coats about them, the Three Magi of the Orient appeared at the door ready to mount their camels.

"How beautiful and handsome they are!" said Carlos to the other stable boys as they held the camels for the Magi to mount.

Large parcels of food and pastries, jugs of water, and innumerable baskets full of all kinds of toys were brought out and tied tightly on the camels' backs. They were soon off while the servants waved and wished them good luck.

On and on they went. As they entered the desert, night fell.

"Dark and somber indeed is the night," said King Gaspar.

"Fear not," remarked King Melchor, "the star will soon appear to guide us as it appears every year: the same star that led us twenty centuries ago to the stable at Bethlehem."

He had hardly finished talking when up above their heads appeared a strange star glittering in the dark.

"Here is the star," said King Melchor again.

"Seems to me," said King Baltazar, "that on our last journey the star always appeared much later; however, I may have lost all sense of time."

They followed the course it led...On and on they went. For hours they travelled.

Suddenly, from behind a cloud a ray of light appeared and darkness gave way to daylight. The sun came out and the strange star disappeared.

Slowly the Three Magi pulled up their reins. "Alas," they exclaimed, "what is the meaning of this?" To their great surprise, after having ridden away in the night, they were standing at their very door—the door of their own castle.

250

"What can this mean?" asked King Gaspar.

"It means," answered King Melchor, "that in the course of the evening we have come back to our starting point."

"But we followed the star," said King Baltazar, in a doleful voice.

"That was no star," piped a small voice.

"Wh-who speaks?" called out King Baltazar—this time in an excited voice.

"Oh, only me," said a little black beetle, coming out from one of the camel's ears.

"You!" cried King Melchor. "How do you know...?"

"Tell us, little beetle, tell us all you know," said King Gaspar.

"The star," said the little beetle, trying to raise its voice loud enough for them to hear, "was just a number of fireflies in formation to imitate a star."

"What are we to do?" moaned King Melchor. "We will never reach Spain. *For the first time the children will find their shoes empty.* What are we to do?"

"Shush—" said the beetle. "Look!"

Toward them, running so fast his thin legs scarcely touched the ground, was coming a little gray mouse.

"Ratón Perez!" exclaimed the Kings.

"My Kings," said Ratón Perez, "it's all the fault of the horses. They are very jealous. While they discussed their plans with the fireflies, I chanced to be resting on a bundle of straw. Too late to follow you, I thought of a plan to undo the fireflies' work. What could be easier than to ask Father Time? It was, as you know, a question of time and only he could arrange it. To my great surprise, I found Father Time sound asleep over his great clock. Not to cause him the least discomfort, lest I should wake him, I set his clock twenty-four hours back. So now, my good Magi, ride on! The children of Spain must have their toys."

As if led by an invisible hand, the three camels pricked up their ears, raised their heads, and went on towards the desert. Silence descended upon the group again. Above them the blue sky and all around them the sand, hot like fire under the rays of the sun. The Magi looked at each other in silence and set their eyes on the road.

Darkness soon closed in. On and on the camels went. They could hardly see themselves in the darkness that enveloped them.

Suddenly a star appeared, large and resplendent, way up in the sky. Its light shone like a silver thread on the sand. In great silence, the Three Magi raised their heads to the sky, and gazed long at the star. There was hope and faith in the three eager faces that now bent their heads to urge the camels on.

From somewhere a sound of bells was heard, faintly at first, then louder and louder.

"God be praised," said King Baltazar, "we are near the city. It's the tolling of the bells—the bells from the church tower, ringing as a reminder of the entrance at Bethlehem years ago, letting us know, as they always do, that we are close to the city gates."

Ding—Dong—Ding—Dong.

The bells chimed now merrily and the hour of twelve struck out. The camels shook their heads, making all their headgear tinkle. Strangely enough, they picked up the tempo of the bells and almost in unison passed the opened gate into the city.

That morning under each bed, inside each shoe, beside baskets and boxes wrapped with straw and flowers, the children found their gifts, unaware of the hardships the Three Magi had in keeping faith with them.

A Christmas Wish

Traditional

God bless the master of this house,
    The mistress also,
And all the little children,
    That round the table go,
And all your kin and kinsmen
    That dwell both far and near;
I wish you a Merry Christmas
    And a Happy New Year.

Index

Titles of stories and poems are in italics. Quotation marks are used to identify first lines of poems. Holiday references are to the entire unit, including the introduction.

Library of Congress Cataloging in Publication Data

Main entry under title:

Holiday ring.

Includes index.
SUMMARY: An anthology of stories, essays, and poetry relating to the major United States and Canadian holidays.
1. Holidays—Juvenile fiction. 2. Holidays—Juvenile poetry. [1. Holidays—Fiction. 2. Holidays—Poetry. 3. Literature—Collections] I. Corrigan, Adeline. II. Bennett, Rainey.

PZ5.H723   [Fic]   75-15975
ISBN 0-8075-3356-4